ESTABLISHED

ALSO BY THE DARK ANGELS COLLECTIVE

Keeping Mum

LESSONS FROM THE WORLD'S OLDEST COMPANIES

by the Dark Angels collective

Unbound

This edition first published in 2018

Unbound
6th Floor Mutual House, 70 Conduit Street, London W1S 2GF

www.unbound.com

Design by Cai and Kyn

A CIP record for this book is available from the British Library

ISBN 978-1-78352-465-5 (trade hbk)
ISBN 978-1-78352-466-2 (ebook)
ISBN 978-1-78352-464-8 (limited edition)

Printed in Great Britain by Clays Ltd, St Ives Plc

1 3 5 7 9 8 6 4 2

In memory of Neil Duffy, 1969-2017
Dark Angel, writer, friend

Dear Reader,

The book you are holding came about in a rather different way to most others. It was funded directly by readers through a new website: Unbound. Unbound is the creation of three writers. We started the company because we believed there had to be a better deal for both writers and readers. On the Unbound website, authors share the ideas for the books they want to write directly with readers. If enough of you support the book by pledging for it in advance, we produce a beautifully bound special subscribers' edition and distribute a regular edition and ebook wherever books are sold, in shops and online.

This new way of publishing is actually a very old idea (Samuel Johnson funded his dictionary this way). We're just using the internet to build each writer a network of patrons. At the back of this book, you'll find the names of all the people who made it happen.

Publishing in this way means readers are no longer just passive consumers of the books they buy, and authors are free to write the books they really want. They get a much fairer return too - half the profits their books generate, rather than a tiny percentage of the cover price.

If you're not yet a subscriber, we hope that you'll want to join our publishing revolution and have your name listed in one of our books in the future. To get you started, here is a £5 discount on your first pledge. Just visit unbound.com, make your pledge and type **established5** in the promo code box when you check out.

Thank you for your support,

Dan, Justin and John
Founders, Unbound

CONTENTS

FOREWORD

Peter Day

Only in fairy stories do people live happily ever after. The rest of us - like the best novels - have a beginning, a middle and an end. And though they try to behave as though it isn't so, the same things happen to companies and organisations.

Success is no guarantee of long-term survival. Indeed, you might say that success sows the seeds of its own destruction. It tends to create a carapace of self-regard that begins to insulate a successful organisation from the world in which it is trying to make its living. Eventually fatally so.

But just a few organisations defy the odds. Of the hundreds of companies I've encountered in decades of reporting, I remember in particular the traditional Japanese inn whose family had been running the place for forty-six generations, some 1,300 years. No surprise that it was in Japan, where they revere crafts, skills and tradition, and often spurn organisational growth and financial engineering.

On a different scale of longevity, one of the most impressive retailers I've encountered in Britain is Booths. It's a small, family-owned grocery chain based in northwestern England, still very proud of its origins as a tea shop in Blackpool in 1847.

In a world of supermarket giants, Booths has stayed true to its roots, and close to its customers. Airy, stylish stores, strong links to local suppliers, and run by Edwin Booth, the great-great-grandson of the founder. With a confident side-swipe at a prominent competitor, Booths' cloth carrier bags declare in bold type: 'Preston not Heston', or 'Cumbria not Umbria'.

But it is more than just slogans. The businesses in this book have memorable stories to tell, and this enthusiasm for corporate story-telling is why I pricked up my ears when I first heard about Dark Angels more than six years ago, and made an *In Business* programme about them on BBC Radio 4.

Great big corporations have a lot to learn from the compelling narratives in *Established,* most of which are about smaller companies. For these potent stories, the big boys can only substitute expensively devised and promoted brands. The tales told in this book are not fairy stories, but they are equally compelling.

Peter Day worked for BBC Radio for more than forty years. He reported on companies large and small for the *Financial World Tonight, Today, In Business* and *Global Business* on the BBC World Service.

INTRODUCTION

Stuart Delves

8/9 November 2016. The first snowfall here in Scotland. An either/or event. It can seem wondrous. It can seem bleak. We heard this day that *Established* had reached its crowd-funding target.

We heard this day also that Donald Trump had been elected the forty-fifth President of the United States of America. The election campaign was long, hard, ugly and vituperative. The result, for many of us, is bleak. A dark winter.

But you might be reading this in a different season. Who knows, there might even be the whiff of optimism in the air. Perhaps that, above all, is the quality you need to survive a long time in business.

Among these momentous tidings, something small but maybe not insignificant. Putting on my shoes to go out and face the uncertain world, I found a Buddhist lapel pin stuck to my rubber sole. On what random centimetre of pavement or worn carpet it lay lost I have no idea. But somewhere in my peram-bulations it stuck to me – a tiny reminder of something bigger, deeper, more enduring than the swings from left to right, or as Brecht said in *The Resistible Rise of Arturo Ui*, 'the bitch being on heat again'.

Established is a book about some of the world's oldest surviving businesses. Businesses that have withstood war, plague, rebellion, boom, bust, depression. The idea for it came to me several years ago while looking at a list of the world's oldest businesses with some, in Japan, going back to the year

578 (a construction company and a hostelry). I thought that was remarkable and almost like something out of the world of fantasy fiction, like Gringotts in Harry Potter. Religions, universities – yes. But businesses? Especially when today our experience is that businesses reaching the age of twenty-five are doing damned well. Dark Angels is more than halfway to that target already.

The question 'How on earth have you managed it?' was the one that John Simmons and I thought could guide such a book and when he, Jamie Jauncey and I welcomed nine new associate partners to a gathering at Moniack Mhor in the Scottish Highlands over the summer solstice in 2015, we thought that co-writing such a business book could be one of several markers of the new phase of Dark Angels. And we opted for English-speaking countries, so, sadly, the salt mines of Poland, the breweries of Belgium and the ceremonial papermakers of Japan fell out of the equation.

Stories, as Dark Angels has banged on about for more than a dozen years now, are the best vehicles for vital information, insights, life lessons. We still learn about what it is to be human from the Greek myths or Shakespeare's plays. We can certainly learn a thing or two about business survival from those that have lasted a couple of hundred years or more. And just as with which myth speaks to you the most, the question for each reader of *Established* is, which story resonates most with yours and what endorsement or caution can you take from it?

So, here it is. *Established*. Twelve great stories. Each of us asking that question of one of twelve disparate companies, from the tiny to the global, all of which have survived for at least a hundred years or more. My village pub was established in 1792 and frankly I don't know how it keeps going! Even in our time here – eighteen years – it's had a run of rum managers including chair-leg-wielding brawlers, absentees, coke dealers and arsonists. Recently its fortunes have changed in the surer hands of Rosie and Kenny, who've embraced the pub's literary associations (in preference to its witchcraft ones), spruced it up and won the first Pub Hub award in Scotland. What would their answer be? Sheer luck probably. And a good roadside location. I hope you enjoy these twelve stories, where longevity comes in many different guises.

IF THESE WALLS
COULD TALK

Gillian Colhoun

ON 20 SEPTEMBER 1803, the patriot and romantic hero of lost causes Robert Emmet was hanged and beheaded in Thomas Street, Dublin, just half a mile away from his former lodgings at the Brazen Head. Found guilty of high treason after leading an unsuccessful revolution against British rule, he was the last to receive this medieval sentence from a British court in Ireland.

It is said that when the executioner asked the twenty-five-year-old revolutionary if he was ready to be hanged, his reply was 'Not yet!' After a pause he asked again, 'Are you ready, sir?' Again Emmet replied, 'Not yet.' By the third time of asking, the hangman had grown impatient, and without further delay went about his brutal business. Emmet's body was taken down after hanging for thirty minutes. He died slowly because of his light frame. The hangman then severed his head with a large blade on a deal block borrowed from a local butcher. Grasping it by the hair, he held it high above the crowd, declaring, 'Behold, the head of a traitor, Robert Emmet.' The bloodied block was displayed for two days in Thomas Street.

While many more characters would come to play their parts in Ireland's tumultuous history, the precipitous death of Robert

Emmet ensured he was rapidly elevated into the pantheon of republican heroes.

Youth, impassioned speeches and a love affair that kept him in Ireland when he could have fled to France only add to the romance. Born in Dublin in 1778 into an affluent Protestant family, Emmet grew up embracing the ideas of fraternity and equality. Like his elder brother Thomas, he became involved with the United Irishmen, an organisation determined to achieve Roman Catholic emancipation and, with Protestant cooperation, an end to British Rule in Ireland. At one time, it was a popular mass movement, but after an unsuccessful rebellion in 1798 the United Irishmen had become an underground elite characterised by high levels of clandestine conspiracy, enemy infiltration, secret codes, invisible ink and various alliances with the French.

A prime location for plotting against British Rule, the Brazen Head in Lower Bridge Street was close to Dublin Castle, the seat of English power in Ireland and the United Irishmen's main target for attack. Its proximity to the quay, the churches and the law courts also made it a hotbed of gossip and an ideal place for strangers to pass on their intelligence in secret. Robert Emmet kept a room in the Brazen Head, just by the main door, so that enemies would be easily spotted and dealt with accordingly.

For all Emmet's careful planning, his hand was forced in July 1803 when an explosion compelled an early call for insurrection. After a haphazard rebellion, that turned out to be little more than a calamitous, bloody riot in Thomas Street, all was lost. Emmet, after fleeing to a safe house in the Wicklow Mountains, was subsequently arrested, tried for treason and put to death along with fifteen of his followers. The hangman, it is said, was also a regular patron of the Brazen Head.

When I arrive at the pub it's four in the afternoon. A painted scroll proudly announces I'm entering the Brazen Head, Ireland's oldest pub, established 1198. I have read of one pub in Athlone, in the west, that claims to date back to 900, but then what's a couple of hundred years when you're within sipping distance of a millennium?

At that time of day, the pleasant courtyard is full of chatter. It's mostly German and American, blandished no doubt by velvety pints of Guinness and what they call here Irish cider. Lovely it is, that holiday-inspired, guilt-free afternoon drinking.

Doors with knobbly glass and long brass handles lead off in different directions. Following my nose, I end up in a bar half the size of any respectable grandmother's front room. The low ceiling makes the room seem dark, but it's cosy. A suited young man is seated at a small table where he eats his bowl of stew and reads his paper. A couple scroll silently through photographs on their iPhones. Another group in the corner is eating chips from a single plate. To the left of them sits an ancient typewriter, a not-so-gentle nod to the pub's literary credentials. The likes of Jonathan Swift and Brendan Behan have all enjoyed the inn's hospitality at one time or another.

There's a grandfather clock guarding the walls, which are papered in beer mats and banknotes. Secrets, too, no doubt, if we are to believe the cast of characters said to have plotted, scribed and drunk here.

Random objects of dubious origin hang from the ceiling – a bodhrán drum, a samurai sword, a bugle – just three items that invite all sorts of questions. The wooden bar stools have red leather tops cratered like the surface of Mars, worn through over the years, caressed by the backsides of the wildly famous and the

Wall mural.

perfectly ordinary. And like any Irish pub that knows its worth, an obligatory star-spangled banner, albeit a tiny one, waves at me from behind the ear of a bronze animal, species unknown.

An American approaches the bar and asks for a Barry's tea. A decaf Barry's tea. The barman laughs and so do I. 'No, no decaf,' he says, 'just regular tea.' We laugh because the Brazen Head is no place for decaffeinated anything. It is a maximum-strength, full-throttle, high-octane piece of Dublin history. A renowned rebel pub where Robert Emmet was not the only revolutionary to seek refuge from the authorities. Later, the United Irishmen of 1916 and the leaders of the War of Independence, including Michael Collins, gathered here for meetings to plan the revolution. It has strong literary and musical links, too. As Dean of Saint Patrick's Church, Swift would have walked past the pub every day. He writes in his letters, 'Here only, at the sign of the Brazen Head, are to be sold places and pensions: beware of counterfeits, and take care of mistaking the door.' A favourite haunt of Flann O'Brien and James Joyce, it even appears in *Ulysses*, when the vagrant, Corley, tells Stephen Dedalus and Bloom that at the Brazen Head one can get 'a decent enough do for a bob'.

The Brazen Head no longer offers lodgings, and these days there's nowhere to keep your horse, but its landlord is still serving up award-winning food, drink and tall tales. With storytelling nights currently at number one on Tripadvisor's list of Dublin tourism attractions and a permanent fixture on every one of 'Ireland's best pub' listings, the Brazen Head seems to be as successful and popular as it ever was.

Today, it is owned by John Hoyne, a man who twelve years ago could no longer watch his favourite bar fall deeper into neglect. He tells me, 'I was born two miles away. I went to school round here, celebrated my eighteenth, twenty-first and fiftieth birthdays in this pub. The former landlord ran the place well enough but there's no doubt it needed some TLC. When it came up for sale, I knew in my heart I could rescue it. And so I did. The Brazen Head is everything. To me, to the staff and the regulars. I call it the centre of the universe, for that is what it is. My job isn't to change, but improve and look after it.'

Hoyne is not a common family name in Ireland and perhaps it's no coincidence that John can trace it all the way back to court jesters of the Kings of Ireland. John's father was a pub landlord and so, with a natural affinity for entertaining, the family has established a successful line in hospitality and pub management. His company owns a number of pubs in the city, but none of them are as important to John as the Brazen Head. 'It's the standard, you see. It's the one that every Irish pub in the world aspires to being,' he tells me. 'Don't get me wrong, everyone thinks their local is the best and for them it is. But for me, and for many others, I'm glad to say, there is something special in these walls. It might be the age of the place, but there is an energy here that is different. It's not something you can quantify with words, it's something you feel.'

We joke about the ghost of Mary Cooney, a former and formidable landlady, keeping a watchful, and critical, eye on them all. But considering the events this place has seen, it would be surprising if they hadn't left something of their own imprints. And that is largely down to geography. Draw a ring around the most important landmarks of historical Dublin – Christchurch Cathedral, Dublin Castle, the Four Courts and Church Street Bridge – and right at its centre you'll find the Brazen Head. A stone's throw from the River Liffey, it is likely that there has been an inn here since as early as the eighth

John Hoyne, owner.

century, and it would have played a vital role in sustaining visitors and their horses on their way to and from the city. Having battled the seas to claim the River Liffey, the Vikings constructed a timber-frame bridge where nine warriors were slaughtered after fleeing back to the city from the Battle of Clontarf. This ancient access point to the then flourishing town was known as the 'Ford of the Hurdles', and the original crossing point on the Liffey that gives its Irish name to Dublin (Baile Átha Cliath, meaning 'Town of the Hurdled Ford'). Maintained and rebuilt over centuries, the bridge carried all pedestrians, livestock and horse-drawn traffic across the river and into the city.

How the pub was given its name is open to interpretation. One theory goes that during one of the many rebellions against English rule an overly curious redhead stuck her head out of the pub window to observe the action on the streets below. When a cannon ball was fired by the Williamite army, it 'removed the head of this well-known red-haired girl of ill-repute'. Apparently, the pub was renamed to commemorate her hapless curiosity.

Little is known about the early proprietors of the bar. On 30 June 1922, the Public Records Office housed in Dublin's Four Courts building, just a few hundred yards away, went up in smoke. After two days of bombing, an explosion and a fire ravaged the building and destroyed many irreplaceable records, census reports and parish registers. The attack marked the beginning of the Irish Civil War.

'We don't know much about the families who owned and managed the place,' John explains. 'I do know that in later years it was run mostly by women, and with an iron fist, too. There was a time when it had real status, the Shelbourne Hotel of its day, if you like.' He tells me a story about Mary Cooney when she was very much alive. A letter had arrived from *Life* magazine asking her to forward a history of the pub, interesting legends and speciality cocktail recipes. This was for a guide the magazine was producing on the world's greatest bars. On passing the letter round to her group of regulars, she asked, 'Well now, what do you make of that?' To which a man in the corner with a thick Cavan accent replied, 'I wouldn't tell the feckers anything.' And neither she did.

Since John Hoyne has taken the reins, he has increased revenue by almost 70 per cent. How has he managed it, especially in a time when most landlords would happily call last orders for good if the banks would let them? In the last decade, more than 2,000 Irish pubs have closed. While many have been casualties of changing lifestyles and drinking habits, this still seems like a large number considering their importance to the country's tourism economy.

John has somehow managed to thrive by appearing to change very little. 'What I try to do is give customers what they want. We have a few antiquities here, such as Emmet's writing desk and his three-person chair; and we're trying to replicate his room and others so that people can get a real sense of how they lived. Food is crucial to this business and we try to keep things simple but delicious. The biggest factor is the quality of my staff. My two managers have been with me for over twenty years. My daughters and my son work full time in the business. Doing things the right way, our way, is personal to us all.

'We've introduced storytelling evenings which have become incredibly popular. Ten years ago, we started with eight people around a dinner table. We served up authentic Irish food, threw in some fairy folklore. Now we have a hundred people a

The Back Bar.

night. We decorate the rooms, the waiting staff are all trained to do things in a certain way. We have traditional live music. It's like a wedding and people have a great time, but we run it like clockwork. Everything is planned in meticulous detail.'

It's not all tourism-focused either. The Brazen Head has a loyal local following, too. 'I love our regulars,' John says. 'They all have their own stools over there. We call it Nuts' Corner. They're like the United Nations with all nationalities represented. Honestly, they probably know more about this place than I do. People come in and listen to their stories. It's real. But at the end of the day, someone has to be captain of the ship. And that's no different from any business. There needs to be a clear vision and purpose, but it takes strong leadership to make that happen.'

Listening to John, I can't help but compare his love for this extraordinary place with the often vacuous professions of passion we hear so much these days. 'Passion' is a word in danger of losing its ardour. We are becoming a society of passionate people, passionately pursuing our passions; and while it is true that enthusiasm for any endeavour is a good thing, this desire to say how passionate we are is at odds with the original meaning of the word – 'suffering'. Do we care for anything so much that we are willing to suffer for it? As I think about this, I return to John's observation that, for him, the Brazen Head is not really about business at all. His feelings for it are not just personal, but elemental, and he'll stop at nothing to keep it in his life. He gives me a guided tour of every room and explains every detail, every painting with pride and knowledge. Has he suffered to make it this successful? Certainly not in the martyrdom sense, but the Irish economy has been savage; and yet twice, having been offered at least double what he paid for the place, John has declined without hesitation. 'I'd never sell it, you see. It's not vanity. But this place is as much my story as it is Emmet's or Collins' or Dublin's for that matter; I want it to be part of the Hoyne family story for generations to come.'

John Hoyne proves the rule that the difference between the good and the truly great bars of the world is the landlord. Like all great public houses, the place is an extension of his personality; and the converse of this is the reason why pub chains don't really work.

Old buildings have a character that attracts people; they just do. In the case of the Brazen Head, it's something to do with the warm timber, the decorative glass and awkward corners – and something more. As John says, 'There is no chance to renovate or to save a historic site once it's gone.' And who knows what society will value in the future. No one feels this more than John. He says he isn't the owner, but the custodian. A fit-looking man now in his fifties, he shows no signs of slowing down. Twenty years from now, if anyone should ask him if he's ready to retire, I'd guess the response would be, 'Not yet, my friend ... not yet.'

The importance of the Brazen Head in Dublin's political and cultural history has been mythologised, eulogised even, and rightly so. From its twelfth-century customers to today's American tourists, it has never wanted for passing trade. Many times it could have burned down or been blown to smithereens, but as a refuge for writers and artists, heroes and villains, neither the British nor the rebels would have closed its doors – it was just too good a source of information.

As for Robert Emmet, though his short, dramatic life came to a tragic end, his passion for an Irish republic left its mark. His defiance transcended the inglorious failure of 1803 – a defiance that captures the spirit of the Brazen Head and its landlord's persistence to protect its legacy, no matter what.

The Courtyard.

2

UPLIFTING

Stuart Delves

I MAGINE, FOR A BRIEF MOMENT, you're a superhero. Along with other powers, you have X-ray vision. There are miles and miles of fun in this. Quite apart from being able to tell your hot date what colour knickers they're wearing, you can see through the steel or tarpaulin sides of articulated and rigid pantechnicons and curtain haulage wagons. Specifically, you can see through the distinctive navy blue sides of any of the thirty-five-strong fleet of Aberdeen's Shore Porters' Society and, indeed, through the protective fawn blankets. On any one day, or night, along the M90, the M8, the M6, the M62, the M1, the M25, or the B9077, you might see:

Entire households (from armchairs to xylophones)

A car

Chinese porcelain

MRI machines

Carrots

Christmas trees

Drilling pipes (for oil)

A stowaway cat

A boat

A chicken coop

White goods

Logs

Pianos

Potatoes

Peat

Ashes	Bank safes
Skis	Books, bibles
Documents	A consignment of stuffed
Paintings	animal heads (stags, otters, stoats, a squirrel).

And once upon a time, but not now, you might have spotted surgical waste. [*Spare the details.*] And, once upon another time, if you'd happened to see the mortuary run you'd have been down the intergalactic pawnbrokers in a flash, trading in those X-ray powers. You might even have swapped them for the sensible and very reasonable viewpoint of the woman in Hertfordshire who phoned head office in the spirit of being a good citizen to say she'd spotted a typo on the side of a Shore Porters' lorry parked up for a house clearance down her street. Surely it should be Established 1948 not [*muffled laughter*] Established 1498! Why, that was before – oh I don't know – Henry VIII and all that carry on.

Once upon a time, in this company's long history (a cool 518 years, from Christopher Columbus to Co-mission Cosmonauts) there were no trucks, no light delivery or 7.5 tonne vans, no juggernauts. There were horses. And carts. And stables with haylofts a furlong in from the harbour quayside. And, preceding that, loading bundles of hide and wool and barrels of salted fish from rowing boat to ship's deck and wine and silk and oranges from rowing boat to wharf, the strong-armed Pynours, men and women both, assisted with the traffic of goods through the already long-established Aberdeen Harbour.

1136 is the date the Harbour, itself still a going concern, was established by King David I of Scotland and it's more than likely that Warkmen and Warkwomen – Porters at the Shore

- were working as long as there were cargo ships to load and unload. In fact the first Pynour (a word of Middle Dutch origin generally held to mean 'carrier of goods'), one John Henrysoun, is on record as 'joining' in 1467 before the formation of what was, in time, to become The Shore Porters' Society. Other early 'joiners' had a wonderful array of names including Gelis Gray, Canny Dog, Megy Tod and Hungre Jok.

The work required great strength. Strength that would have even Clark Kent or Black Widow raising an eyebrow. A Council extract of April 1636 states that before a man or woman can become a labourer of 'the Shoar' they must first pass a test of strength. The Town Water Bailie adjudicated, and successful candidates were licensed by the Magistrates. The test was to carry one hundredweight on the back from the Harbour Mouth to the Braid Gutter - a distance of about one mile - without resting. One Porter (or member) is on record as having carried a package weighing six hundredweight on his back from the cart and up several flights of stairs to an upper floor of a warehouse. Generally, though, the official maximum weight for one man was one hundredweight, known as a 'birne' or man's lift, greater weights being shared, with notes of twa men's lifts, four, six and eight men's lifts. Before wheeled vehicles were introduced one method of carrying, first cited in 1701, was to sling goods on a stout pole which was carried on the men's shoulders: this was known as the sting lift. In the earlier centuries it seems that women may well have taken part in these feats but after about 1650 they no longer appear in the records.

In his book celebrating the Society's 500th anniversary, George Gordon writes: 'Most probably starting as a group with kindred interests and associations banding themselves together for their mutual protection, the old Pynours founded

Shore Porters pulling their weight.

what must be one of the oldest co-operatives in existence. In character the Society has changed but little, the mutual element is ever present, though in modern business parlance it is now a Private Partnership. There are no outside shareholders or other interested parties.'

In 1666 as sparks spat into a callous wind through London, up north in the Granite City the Superannuated Members Fund, or Property and Warehousing Department, was founded as one of two distinct trading units to provide for retired and sick partners. The other unit was known as the General Haulage Department, the Horse and Van Department, or simply the Working Department.

For centuries the Pynours were a semi-public body under the control of the Town Council of Aberdeen but gradually over the years, because of changing conditions, the association became less strong and in about 1850 they became completely independent. They became known as The Shore Porters' Society in 1836.

The mainstays of trade changed through the centuries as well, with linen and whaling being the dominant commodities in the 1700s (whale oil and blubber were used for lighting lamps), granite and shipbuilding taking precedence in the 1800s. The focus of the company changed, too, from portering to warehousing and the transportation of goods via the UK's road system. Always a thriving commercial hub, since 1964 Aberdeen has been the Oil Capital of Europe, though that too is now changing fast.

When I met Kevin Brown, one of today's Partners, on a cold November day that threatened sleet and early flaughts, with the lack of sun eliciting bleakness rather than sparkle out of the city's granite architecture, he spoke of the effects of the slump in oil prices on the Aberdeen economy and community. Half-deserted hotels. Whispering restaurants. Idling taxi drivers. Executive villas rented out to students. All-expenses-paid company men having to fish out their own credit cards.

But although the yard of their new state-of-the-art warehouse is stacked with drilling pipes and for many years they have moved the household effects of oilmen into and out of Aberdeen, the Society has never become reliant on the oil industry for its survival. Then I suppose, alongside the time-span that the inscribed parchment of old animal hide that was lying on the boardroom table represents, a forty years' boom is but a chapter or a phase. (The parchment – ancient title deeds inscribed in Latin – had been brought out of safekeeping, not for my benefit but for perusal by a curator from Aberdeen Museum: unsurprisingly the company's heritage is of perennial interest.)

As we sat in the panelled boardroom with two carved chairs – one the Horse Master's, the other the Deacon's – conveying ever so slightly a sense of medieval ritualism, Kevin provided some insights into the complexities and challenges of modern-day transportation. Today the Working Department trades as International Removers and Hauliers and operates out of Aberdeen and Richmond-upon-Thames, south-west London, with a fleet of thirty-five lorries and vans. Fifty to 60 per cent of business consists of the shifting and storage of personal effects. Loads – whether personal effects or goods – bound for abroad either go to the UK's main ports of Grangemouth, Tilbury, Felixstowe, Hull, Southampton and Aberdeen itself, or via air. Paperwork and security measures are extensive. 'The biggest catalyst for changing borders and how shipping is done has been 9/11,' confirmed Kevin.

We nod. We know. The world has changed. Shackled by bureaucracy. But among the litany of red tape some specifics glittered and caught my attention, as I'm sure Kevin intended. It wasn't just the corporate line of business benefit # 4: 'We keep up with the regs'.

INTERESTING FREIGHT FACT 1: All batteries have to be disconnected/removed from goods in transit by air.

INTERESTING FREIGHT FACT 2: Outside gardening equipment like forks, trowels, rakes and hoes bound for Oz have to be spotlessly clean. They've got enough bugs and insects of their own.

INTERESTING FREIGHT FACT 3: Antiques containing any amount of ivory are subject to all sorts of permits.

INTERESTING FREIGHT FACT 4: Regarding taxidermy and trophy heads, airlines now refuse to carry them. That poses a bit of a problem for all the Swedish and German hunters who come to enjoy Scotland's wilderness sports.

And, yes, wait a minute, regarding taxidermy and trophy heads, what was the story behind the consignment of stuffed animal heads? Where had they come from and where were they bound? 'Ah,' smiled Kevin. 'They were from a hotel in Helmsdale. There were over a hundred of them, mostly adorning the walls of the residents' lounge; or with the little beasts, bodies intact, glaring down from the mantelpiece or gleaming up from beside the fireguards. As you may know, Helmsdale is an attractive coastal village on the dramatic road north through Sutherland and a lot of people stop off and stay over. The hotel's new proprietors were at a loss as to why guest after guest would check in, start to settle in, then next thing they knew, they were checking out. Then they clocked. It was the eyes. The ubiquitous eyes. And the hectare of dried hide. So, they got rid of them. They went for sale.'

From the outside many businesses, professions, trades look, well, dull, mechanical, monotonous. Until you hear the stories. And, of course, removals provide an insight into people's lives, their 'stuff', and often take place at significant junctures and crisis points like divorce and death. As you might expect, they've had the police round too on several occasions, reclaiming stolen goods sitting innocently in storage. So stories abound. Not that Kevin wasn't acutely aware of the issues of privacy and confidentiality. So he didn't tell me about the high court judge with wardrobes and clothes horses of dresses or the agony aunt with a fully stocked gun room. (He really didn't, I made that up.) But he did tell me about the chicken coop. And Bob's ashes. And the stack of wheelie bins in Warehouse I.

Now, if you really had the super-duper version of the X-ray eyes and happened across the consignment in question you'd have not only seen through the side of the truck, you'd have not only seen through the coddling blanket, you'd have seen through the wooden panels of the chicken coop, and seen – the clucking chickens themselves. You could have tipped off the owner. She was in a terrible state. She had no idea where her chickens were. They were supposed to be in her garden but they'd crept back into the coop dormitory before the whole thing was lifted into the truck, so were in transit unbeknownst to anybody. It all ended well, of course, though history doesn't recount whether there were any eggs at the end of the journey.

The shore and beyond.

Only you, Captain America, could have reported whether any eggs were still within.

Bob's ashes. Here's the thing. Whenever a Shore Porter handles and moves a valuable item he affixes a sticker bearing his name, just in case anything goes wrong or gets broken. (Business benefit # 6: Accountability.) A client's husband's ashes are without question a valuable item. The porter who handled the urn was called Bob. So was the client's deceased husband. When the lorry-load of effects arrived at her new flat and the client came across her husband's urn she was really touched – they'd written his name on the side. How sweet. And she phoned in to say not only how pleased she was with the service but also how thoughtful this little demonstration of respect was. 'Except,' she added, 'he really preferred to be called by his proper name – Robert.'

Kevin showed me around two of the company's warehouses in Aberdeen. One we passed and didn't go into was the old stable block. In all the Society has over 212,000 square feet of storage at its disposal. In the newest hi-tech warehouse, with sophisticated computerised tracking systems, commercial products like packaging and chemicals were being stored that biting November afternoon. The other was another more ramshackle world with the ghostly air of a grand country house in winter – everyone away and the sofas and dressing tables under dust-sheets. There were 'shapes' we passed that Kevin deciphered but forbade me from mentioning. Nothing sinister or illegal, just some very bizarre belongings. 'You see all kinds,' I commented. 'The whole gamut,' he replied. The bizarre consignment I am allowed to mention was two towers of large black wheelie bins stacked one inside the other. 'Bound for Arkansas.' 'Anything else going?' I asked. 'No. Just the bins. The client has a place in the desert.' The mind boggles. It's been said before but it's true: there's nowt so queer as folk.

Are the Shore Porters odd? They're certainly different and have a distinct business model. Who's this Deacon for a start? A rotating honorary position that has the casting vote not once used in the last twenty years. Ah, and … Kevin did then proceed to tell me about the intricacies of the Society, signing up to a set of rules dating back to the 1800s, doing at least twenty-one years of service before being considered to be a partner, the differences between the Working Department and the Property Department … but really it's its own world in respect of its formation and rules. I'm not sure how much anyone outside can usefully learn from that.

Cutting to the heart of it, though, the winning characteristic of the Society that I drew from what Kevin was saying is commitment and, integral to that, loyalty. Those fifteenth-century Pynours with their 'jaickets and bunnets' grouped together for mutual protection, mutual 'looking out for each other': they committed to each other. That is the energy I sense that has kept this business alive and given a living to so many for so long. Some things change, inevitably, just as horsepower shifted from loins to pistons. The Society members today are not the whole workforce, they are the partners and retired partners. It may no longer, strictly speaking, be a cooperative but commitment through long service can lead to becoming a member and enjoying the protection and benefits that offers. That may not be everybody's cup of tea but for those to whom it is, it is a strong brew. And undoubtedly mutuality, however restrictive that might have become, has been a strength that has counted towards the Society's longevity.

What they have, though, that still works for the good of the whole is a flat management structure, with partners very much hands on. 'All points of view are taken on board – we don't always agree!' A rather astonishing factor but one that's very sound is that the Society operates a three-year probationary period for every member of staff, allowing the individual to get to know the partnership and vice versa (the seedbed of that greater commitment for those who take on the long haul).

There's no nepotism. They've kept to a modest, manageable size. They foster and enjoy good customer relations. 'And we've made many an astute decision along the way over the years,' adds Kevin. What he values is being his own boss and being able to make decisions that change things. And, yes, there's the odd perk like the unwanted TV, microwave or sofa. That extends to everyone!

What's warming – and it was good to leave with a warm feeling to sustain me on the wintry three-hour drive home – is what I'd describe as the humanistic foundation of this company, the Society of Shore Porters. And a real sense of bodily sweat and toil – muscularity – at the core. Turning from the vehicles to the people, those X-ray eyes may not be able to detect a soul – that's metaphysical after all – but they'd certainly see a beating heart – exhilarating in that one hundredweight or more.

3

CUSTARD PIES, KITTY THE SUFFRAGETTE AND A BOAT CALLED BIG LOVE

Elen Lewis

London Hampton Races. The ferry at Moulsey, 1866.

This is the tale of one river and one city.

A tale of liquid history.

This is a tale that sounds like church bells tolling for a king on a golden barge, watermen cussing as they race across the waters, the slap-slap-lapping of the tide against the muddy bank, the ra-ra-wra-ack of the heron's call slicing misty air.

This is a tale that smells damp, of slight salt and wet earth, of underground mushrooms and forests in the rain.

This is a tale marked by tides, currents, swells, storms, rain, the moon, and white chalk on a blackboard.

This is the tale of a ferry that has been crossing the river from Hampton to Molesey since 1514. The oldest ferry on the Thames.

BIG LOVE AND A PIRATE SHIP FOR COOTS

FIVE HUNDRED YEARS LATER and I ring the bell to call the ferryman to take me across the river. It is an old-fashioned bell, weathered green, bigger than my hand, and it hangs from the whitewashed sign with FERRY written in red capital letters across the top like a gateway into another world. The riverbank is quiet and it's hard to believe that this signal will work. It's louder than it looks it might be.

But then he's coming, slowly along the bank from where the houseboats are moored. Blue t-shirt, peaked cap and sunglasses.

'I'll take you across,' he says.

Without asking questions, because why else would I be there? I thought I might need to wait for more passengers to join me but this is a water taxi. It comes when you call.

The boat is small, green, low in the water. It has a jaunty white sign, same red lettering as the bell sign – HAMPTON FERRY. There are two wooden benches on each side and Ben stands in the middle at the back behind a wooden plinth, like a preacher man. He'll take buggies, bikes, dogs, anything really that needs to cross the river. It costs £1.50 for adults, 50p for kids, bikes and buggies.

Ring the bell to call the Hampton Ferry.

Dogs are free. Ben tells me the boat is a retired army assault craft with the luxury of an outboard motor that can carry up to twelve people. I think twelve passengers would feel full.

Ben lives on a canal boat called *BIG LOVE*, painted purple with stars. It's moored in the boatyard next to the yellow rowing boats for hire and some swankier looking motorboats. His houseboat's for sale; he needs more space to start a family with his beautiful girlfriend who calls him 'baby' and lolls in the reeds. From this distance midway across the river, she might be a mermaid or nymph with her long curly hair, olive skin and the way she waves lazily to her waterman from a sunbathing spot on the roof of *BIG LOVE*.

'Don't be long, baby,' her voice drifts across the water.

Ben smiles. 'There are very few better places to be, on a day like today, than on the river.'

Ben likes the element of freedom you get from living on the river. This is his fifth summer here, scratching a living as ferryman. He also carves driftwood and helps to build houseboats. He's the third generation to live near the river; his grandfather built the sailing club, just ten metres away from the ferry, down Benn's Alley, on Benn's Island.

'Is it named Benn's Island after you?'

Ben doesn't answer. 'I went sailing last night as it happens,' he says. 'If I had my own boat I'd skive.'

Ben knows why the Hampton Ferry is one of the oldest businesses in the country.

'Simplicity,' he says. 'It doesn't need a huge amount to keep going' Without the ferry, their regular commuters would need to walk around three miles over Hampton Court Bridge or deal with traffic. 'Road works are good for us,' he says.

But Ben would rather talk about the tiny pirate ship he's

built for the coots' nest from driftwood. It has a cutlass and bobs around on a tyre close to the jetty. 'The coots have hatched now. Last year, what with the floods and that, it was tragic watching the coot trying to keep its nest dry.'

What's the hardest thing about being a ferryman? It's the silly questions, Ben tells me. People don't know which way the sea is. They ask him what river it is. They want to sail to Tower Bridge at six o'clock in the evening.

'A ferryman is supposed to know everything,' he sighs.

The Simplicity of Chalk

Mike Douglas and Dave Bedford, two retired engineers, run the ferry together, paying Ben with a combination of commission and free mooring for his *BIG LOVE* boat.

When Dave was made redundant as a senior engineer in government he wanted something else to do. So when the lease came up he bought the Hampton Boatyard. He took a boat safety course and now also works as a boat safety examiner. Then one afternoon his phone rang when he was halfway across the river.

'The ferryman's run away. Dave, I need someone to run the ferryboat.'

And that was how it started.

This is not a business you go into if you want to make loads of money. Trade is dependent on the weather and the ferry normally takes around £5 a day, but only in British summer time. Last Bank Holiday Monday they took £6.

'I don't think anyone can earn a living,' admits Dave. 'If you wanted it as a viable business you'd shut it down. You have to be here because it's a service to the community. And because it's fun playing with boats.'

Like Ben, Dave lives on the river. We can see his floating

house on the edge of Garrick's Island in the middle of the river and to the left of the ferry's jetty. He's just built a balcony off the bedroom so he and his wife can watch the sun set across the river. His family have lived on the island since the 1920s.

For Mike, working on the ferry represented a new start. In 2007 he had a triple bypass. He's since stopped smoking.

'I'll keep moving, touch wood,' he said. 'And this is a nice place to be. It's not like the roads. There's no stress. We don't have to make a profit, we just need to pay our bills.'

Is this the secret to Hampton Ferry's longevity or is there something else? Mike and Dave remember when a woman rang them up trying to sell a computerised system to help rent out their boats.

'What do you use now?' she said down the phone as they sat at the picnic table outside watching the swell of the river.

'We can't work without chalk,' said Mike. 'Blackboard and chalk. Not a lot goes wrong with a blackboard apart from torrential rain.'

Then he tells me the story of the US space pen and the Russians' pencil. During the space race in the 1960s, legend has it, NASA scientists realised that pens could not function in space. They needed to figure out another way for the astronauts to write things down. So they spent years and millions of taxpayer dollars to develop a pen that could put ink to paper without gravity. But their crafty Soviet counterparts, so the story goes, simply gave their cosmonauts pencils.

'We can't stand complications,' he says.

Crossing the Waters
The stories this Hampton Ferry has witnessed. From Tudor kings, to blood-stained duels, bare-knuckle fighting, hot air

balloons, blazing suffragettes, Lord Byron, Charlie Chaplin – all marked by the bell to call the ferryman.

It's not just about messing around on boats. There has to be a reason to cross the waters. In 1249, the patch of land across the water was called Herstegg, 'lammas land', which means the hay was made in spring and summer and thereafter from 'Lammas Day, the first of August' it was open to commoners to graze cattle until Candlemas Day on the second of February. Later people would cross the river to collect reeds for thatching.

Henry VIII travelled by royal barge from Hampton Court Palace to his palace at Oatlands, Weybridge. The church bells rang as he passed by.

All industries have their good times and bad times. In the eighteenth and nineteenth centuries the river was swarming with boats and ferrymen making good livings. The fierce ferrymen would challenge rivals to rowing races to stay head of the river. On some days you could cross the river by walking from boat to boat. Think Canaletto's Thames.

As a place that was close to town yet sequestered enough to be undisturbed, Moseley Hurst became a favoured spot for duels to settle affairs of honour and prize fighting.

On 1 July 1794, at the 'duel stained sod of Moulsey Hurst' the Earl of Tankerville shot and wounded a married man, Mr Edward Bouverie, who had ignored his warnings not to woo his daughter. They met at dawn and took their stations at a distance of twelve paces. Mr Bouverie declined to fire, but the Earl of Tankerville pointed his pistol, took aim and shot. Bouverie was hit in the abdomen and severely wounded, so much so that *The Times* reported his death. The following week, the newspaper published a retraction. 'We are happy to learn,' it said, 'that the accounts which have been published in this and other newspapers, concerning the Hon. Mr. Bouverie, have been founded in error; so far that they announced his death. We are requested to state that Mr. Bouverie, though very severely wounded, is now in a fair way of recovery. We cannot omit our testimony of the coolness and good conduct displayed by both on this occasion.'

Between 1805 and 1824, there were over a hundred bare-knuckle fights, more than anywhere else in England. One fight lasted eighty-eight minutes over sixty-eight rounds and the men died. Crowds poured onto the land, sometimes as many as 10,000, all jostling for a place near the ringside.

It began by chance on Monday 11 March 1805, when Elias Spray, a coppersmith, was due to fight Henry Pearce, nicknamed 'Hen' or 'The Game chickhen'; and Hampton was selected as the spot for the encounter. The Middlesex magistrates, however, had other views, for prize fighting was illegal and, fearing an interruption from the authorities, the organisers decided to cross over into Surrey, where it seems the justices were thought to take their responsibilities in lighter fashion.

> To see the Hurst with tents encamped on,
> Look around the scene from Hampton.
> 'Tis life to cross the laden ferry,
> With boon companions wild and merry,
> And see the ring upon the Hurst,
> With carts encircled – Hear the burst,
> At distance of the eager crowd.
> Oh! It is life to see a proud
> And dauntless man step, full of hopes,
> Up to the P.R. stakes and ropes,
> Throw in his hat, and, with a spring,
> Get gallantly within the ring.

The *Morning Chronicle* says: 'Considerable confusion took place in procuring boats to convey the numerous followers across the river, where several not only experienced a good ducking, but some narrowly escaped drowning in their eagerness to reach the destined spot.' Another account described the scene: 'By hook or by crook the vast assemblage found themselves on the other side of the Thames and were on Moulsey Hurst, that place destined to see so many engagements in the ring afterwards. This occasion, however, was the very first time that the ropes and stakes were pitched upon that now classic spot; the most celebrated of trysting places connected with the prize ring.'

As the clock on the tower of Hampton Church struck one, the antagonists entered the ring and battered each other for thirty-five minutes and twenty-nine rounds, before Spray's seconds considered he had received enough punishment and threw in the towel on his behalf.

The records of *The Ring* contain accounts of around a hundred fights that took place on the Hurst, and there were dozens more which never found their way into the journals. The fighters had names like Alexander the Coalheaver, the Master of the Rolls (a baker by trade), the Streatham Youth, Holt the Duffer, the Chelsea Snob, the Phenomenon, Scroggins the Sailor, Dutch Sam, the Gaslight man.

It was boom time for the ferrymen. One account talks of people rushing home across the water when the fights were over:

> The night fast approaching, the proverb of the 'devil take the hindmost', seemed to be uppermost. The toddlers brushed off by thousands to the water's edge, and, in spite of the entreaties of the ferrymen, the first rush jumped into the boats in such numbers as nearly to endanger their own lives.

However, the watermen soon got the best of it by demanding
a bob or more to carry over in safety select companies. Yet
so great was the pressure of the crowd, and so eager to cross
the water to Hampton, that several embraced Old Father
Thames against their will, amidst the jeers and shouts of their
more fortunate companions. The other side of the Hurst
produced as much fun and laughter, from the barouches,
rattlers, gigs, heavy drags, etc., galloping off towards Kingston
Bridge through fields covered with water to save time. Several
were seen sticking fast in the mud, the proprietors begging
assistance from those persons whose horses were strong
enough for the purpose. One block up of this kind operated
on a string of carriages upwards of half a mile in length. The
vehicles were so numerous, that two hours had elapsed
before the whole of them had passed over Kingston Bridge,
to the great joy and profit of the proprietors of the gates.

The ferrymen's desire to milk the potential commercial opportunity backfired in June 1819 when Tom Shelton, 'the Navigator',
was due to fight Ben Burn. The local ferrymen, who had a legal
monopoly of the ferry across from the Hurst to Hampton,
refused to share their pickings with the London watermen, and
declined to let them take people across the river. In fact, at a
previous fight they had had several of them fined for doing so;
the watermen had their revenge by informing magistrates that
a fight was going to take place. The fight was moved to Hounslow
Heath and the ferrymen didn't make any money.

With bare-knuckle fighting came horse racing. From 1737
to 1962, Hampton Races attracted crowds of up to 100,000
including, in 1808, the Duke of York and Lord Byron. There
were drinking tents, stalls, bands, fortune tellers, gambling

stalls and sideshows. Gypsies, travellers and hawkers would camp on the land. The number of people meant the races could be a hazardous place and the first lock-keeper at Molesey Lock was killed under the hooves of a racehorse here.

In 1887 the Jockey Club refused to renew the racing licence on the grounds that the course was too dangerous and that was the end of the 'happy Hampton races' – until a purpose-built, fenced racecourse with grandstands and a club house was constructed.

In 1913, Hampton Races became internationally famous when two suffragettes, Clara Giveen and Kitty Marion, set fire to the royal box and the grandstand, both of which were burned to the ground. Each was sentenced to three years in prison. Kitty Marion went on hunger strike and was repeatedly force-fed. Eventually she became so ill she had to be released as the authorities did not want to create a martyr. She had been arrested several times before and said that she had been force-fed 232 times in four hunger strikes. Kitty Marion's tenacity and dedication to the cause made her an important figure in the history of the suffragette movement.

Bridges Over Troubled Water
There's something about living on the Thames. Different rules, different people. 'We all have an affinity with the place,' says Dave the ferryman. 'We just don't get stressed.' He pushes back his baseball cap and waves at a boat as it passes. Later, however, when we talk about the floods and how they damaged business he admits, 'It rains and you're pulling your hair out.'

He tells me that this part of the river attracts three different kinds of people – multimillionaires, rock stars and eccentrics. A raised eyebrow tells me that he is neither millionaire nor rock star. He's not impressed with the millionaires who buy motor-boats, pay for moorings in his boatyard and never use them.

'I've had one boat not go out for ten years,' he says.

My favourite houseboat on this part of the river is *Astoria*, now a recording studio for Pink Floyd's David Gilmour. It is built in ornate wood, like a giant Swiss musical box, and is big enough to house a ninety-piece orchestra. It was built in 1911 for music-hall impresario Fred Karno, who used to entertain his protégé Charlie Chaplin there. Apart from mentoring comedians like Chaplin and Stan Laurel, Karno popularised the custard-pie-in-the face gag.

In 1912, Fred Karno bought Tagg's Island, just downstream, and built a grand hotel called the Karsino. It had a ballroom, with a resident orchestra, that seated 350. Ferries were laid on to take guests to the island and a hundred small boats were provided for their amusement. There was even a Palm Court Concert Pavilion for 650 people with a domed roof painted with views of Hampton Court Palace. At the weekends, the island swarmed with celebrities and society bigwigs. Then came cinema and three summers of bad weather and people stopped coming to the Karsino's music hall. Fred Karno went bankrupt in 1925 and eventually retired to Dorset as part-owner of an off-licence bought with financial help from Charlie Chaplin.

Building Bridges

The Hampton Ferry doesn't have to reinvent itself for fashion and fickle tastes, but its fortunes have ebbed and flowed over the last 500 years, swayed by what's happening on the other side of the river. Horse racing and prize fighting are good for business, a simple park less so. Sunshine is brilliant for boats, rain is not. And in the good old days for the ferrymen there were no bridges between Kingston and Staines along the River Thames. Today, there are 214. But the ferry is still sailing, still going to and fro between the riverbanks, and will continue to do so provided there are ferrymen like Dave and Mike and Ben who are happy to mess around on boats and not seek their fortunes.

'The river is a thread of sanity,' says Dave.

Lives are lived and lost, fortunes swell and disappear. Families come and go. The floods roll in and out. The ferryman crosses the river. The river flows on and on.

'The river is a thread of sanity.'

4

A CUT ABOVE

Martin Lee

*The indenture was made at Bridport on the 12th September 1515,
between William Charde and John Orchard, bailiffs of the aforesaid
borough on one part; and Robert Balson on the other part.*

I MAGINE, IF YOU WILL, that Mr Robert Balson of Bridport, Dorset, on 12 September 1515, were to be granted the gift of time travel, and used it to move precisely 500 years forward in time. We can assume, without fear of contradiction, that everything would astound him. To modern eyes, Bridport is a charming, mildly bustling English provincial market town. It's a great place to live, work and raise a family, having enough scale to provide most needs, but not so large as to be of interest to the biggest colonising brands.

Yet to Balson's boggled vision today's Bridport would be incomprehensibly vast and confusing, a cosmopolitan metropolis nearly a third the size of Henry VIII's London. The modern equivalent would be to fuse, say, Birmingham, Glasgow and Manchester together into one conurbation. Certain things, such as motorised traffic and electric lighting, would instantly confound his bearings. He'd also struggle to make sense of all the writing he could see, or of the businesses on the streets, most of which would be impossible to relate to, even assuming he realised they were commercial premises.

They testify that the aforesaid bailiffs have granted and demised to the aforesaid Robert two shambles situated in˙ the market of the town Bridport.

We can imagine that the first thing he'd do would be to try to locate the market area where his own shambles were situated. It would be an impossible job. The centre of town has been reconfigured beyond recognition over the centuries, and in fact the commercial heart of town has moved as well. For one thing, about 250 years into the life of the Balson butchery business, the current town hall was built, and for many years all the town's butchers (all thirty-seven of them) operated in a covered area on the ground floor, each of them allocated a space of about six square feet. While it's incredible to think of this business as being the longest surviving family business in the UK, it's no mean feat being the longest surviving butcher in Bridport.

As well as the town's prime pitch, in 500 years many other things have also shifted, such as the meaning of the word 'shambles', which nowadays we use metaphorically to refer to anything chaotic and disorderly. From that definition, it's easy to envisage the primitive conditions of an open-air slaughterhouse and meat market, with the runnel in the middle of the butchery space to allow for the offal to be thrown away and the blood to run off.

As our time-travelling Robert continues to stumble around his hometown, he might well happen to walk west, past most of today's shops, over the River Brit and off to the edge of town along the B3162. Here he'd be in for perhaps the biggest shock of

The earlier take on a butcher's window display,
before health and safety legislation kicked in...

all. For however much he'd fail to comprehend modern English, he'd certainly recognise the name of the shop front: R. J. Balson & Son. Possibly, he'd be able to make sense of 'England's oldest family butchers', proudly printed on the butcher's bike propped up outside the shop. As quaintly old-fashioned as the bike looks to us, to him it would be yet another fantastic contraption.

He'd have to walk in, whereupon he'd be confronted by yet more aspects of modernity that would leave him open-mouthed. Of these, the invention of refrigeration is probably the greatest change from the professional butcher's standpoint, along with a level of hygiene and sanitation that might leave him wondering, were it not for the sight of so much meat, if this was still the same trade. And in a sense it's not. In his day, the shambles only operated on a Wednesday and Saturday, and for hundreds of years, until the time when the high street and fixed shops became a feature of our towns, when not in the shambles butchers tended to ply their trade from the public houses on whose premises meat was butchered and sold; for they were also publicans. The Balsons were no different, operating from a good number of pubs over the centuries.

> *Robert is to have and to hold the aforesaid shambles situated in the market for the term of his life paying to the aforesaid bailiffs, and their successors in time to come, five shillings of legal money at the feasts of Easter and St Michael the Archangel (29 September) in equal portions and each Saturday during the year two pence ...*

Once inside the shop, Robert would almost certainly come face to face with the latest Balson to carry the family's torch through history: Richard, the twenty-sixth descendant. What would they

After the difficult first 400 years,
technology finally came to the aid of deliveries ...

say to each other? The deep irony of the licence is that the successors referred to are the bailiffs (of whom history has nothing further to say), rather than the Balson family, the length of whose line of succession puts all British royal houses to shame. Having said that, perhaps we need to give those bailiffs some credit for forward thinking. Had Robert's successors been given the licence in perpetuity, and if it still had legal status today, the current Balson family would now be paying approximately 90p a year in business rates for their fine butchery business.

Apart from the licence, and the careful reconstruction of the entire family tree, the historical record of the Balson business goes cold for some 350 years. From the petulant perspective of the would-be business biographer, this represents a rather short-sighted attitude to legacy building. It's almost as if Balsons 1-20 were interested in nothing more than pleasing customers, and had no eye on creating a famous dynastic business. What we're left with are teasing legends. It's said, for example, that Balson meat went down with the *Mary Rose* as she sailed out of Portsmouth docks in 1545 in front of Henry VIII's eyes.

In fact, scroll forward to 2015 and that relative lack of obsession with legacy is still true. Of course, because we live in an age of data, and pretty much any type of information can be stored with ease, Richard Balson is more able than any of his predecessors to run his shop while simultaneously using the tools of the modern world to spread the story of his family's business. So, the business has a Twitter account, and a book commemorating its 500 years in business, and enters for awards (which it often wins).

Nevertheless, rather like the imagined shock as Robert Balson sees his own name on the door of his time-travel trip to modern Bridport, there is still a shock for today's first-time visitor, especially if, like mine, the purpose of the visit is more bound up with the achievement of a business that is 500 years old than buying meat for the family. And the shock is ... this is a very normal butcher's shop. In fact, the first impression is close to a let-down. It's of average size, it has a regular butcher's window and it has a fifties or sixties pebbledash frontage above the window. It's even off the prime pitch, lying well beyond all the retail in the centre of town.

If you were to enter the shop, unlike the imagined Robert you'd find it all very normal. A long refrigerator with a handsome array of products, especially sausages, a variety of other displays of good food, a clean but regular floor. It's what's *not* there that strikes you. No Merrie Olde England heritage trail kitsch; no butcher's blocks from the seventeenth century and no replica of the original licence. And, indeed, on the day of my visit they would have had more reason than usual to up the volume of history on show, because I turned up on the actual day of the 500th anniversary, and there was literally nothing that would have told you that. The fact is, for all its uniqueness and proud history, it's a working butcher's shop, resolutely operating in the here and now.

It's always delightful to come across an independent shop of any description that has obvious pride in its products and its appearance, but, for all that, I still couldn't work out the secret on first impression. But as I stood in the queue to be served, the secrets that didn't reveal themselves through the bricks and mortar started to appear in the service. All three customers who were served before me were known by name. All were enjoying conversations that sounded like they were starting in the middle, picking up the threads from the previous week, a kind of 'Now, where were we?' All the talk seemed to revolve around meat and family, slipping easily from, say, 'How was that lamb shoulder?' to 'How is Stan's shoulder?' It was a living demonstration of the Balson philosophy that the everyday business of family life is best conducted around the dinner table.

> ... and if it shall happen that the aforesaid rent of five shillings is in arrears for three weeks after the aforesaid feasts or if the aforesaid rent of two pence paid weekly shall be in arrears for a month then the aforesaid bailiffs and their successors shall have the reversion of the aforesaid shambles and the aforesaid Robert Balson shall be expelled, and the aforesaid Robert shall not alienate the shambles without a licence from the bailiffs of the borough under penalty of the year's rent on the shambles, and the aforesaid bailiffs and their successors lease the aforesaid shambles to the aforesaid Robert Balson for the term of his life according to the aforesaid terms.

The other great irony of the original licence is that it ends with a warning of the financial consequences of defaulting. The unmistakable message from the sixteenth century is that business failure was as common then as it is now, and the likelihood of it had to be factored in to any rental agreement. We don't know how many butchery businesses have been and gone in Bridport alone over the last 500 years, but, unbeknownst to the bailiffs, in this instance they were putting the frighteners on the wrong man.

So how have the Balsons done it? With two minor hiccoughs, when the business moved laterally to a brother in one case, and a nephew in the other, it has been an unbroken line of father to son succession for twenty-six generations. If this weren't a business book, it would be just as compelling to look at the genetic stamp of the family, given its ability to keep on generating male heirs, but, sadly, those skills are beyond us.

But, of course, it is the business story we are interested in, and it's a fascinating one. In the telling of it we are indebted to Richard Balson, the current custodian (to use his own self-deprecating description). Understandably, Richard also finds the topic of business longevity interesting, and he's done his own research into it. He's unearthed the statistic that 88 per cent of family business owners believe that the business will still be in family hands in five years' time. However, the reality is otherwise – many of these owners suffer from the optimism bias. The starker truth is that only 30 per cent of family businesses survive into the second generation, and only 3 per cent into the fourth generation. So in the case of Balson & Son, we are in a realm that is inaccessible to statistics. It's tempting to think of it as an almost mystical achievement, or at least it would be if meeting Richard weren't an exercise in listening to one of the most grounded and pragmatic of business people.

Those of us who spend most of our time in business circles are used to watching new ideas for business success coming over the horizon. Many of those ideas have the attraction of novelty, are packed with buzzwords and often come attached to TM processes. It's hard not to get a jaundiced sensation of déjà vu when the latest one hoves into view.

You'll not get any of that from Richard. He preaches traditional virtues, and his language is as muscular as a butcher's forearms. His formula is not a secret, and in fact he's committed his philosophy to the written page. In his own history of the business, he writes this in the final chapter:

The front cover of the book by current owner Richard Balson,
500 Years Behind the Block, celebrating the quincentenary of the business.

For us it is all about the quality of the product and the personal service we offer our customers, many of whom represent families who have been customers for generations. It's about the here and now and planning to succeed. We have a long history, but every generation needs to build on what's been handed down to them, and more importantly be prepared for long hours and plenty of hard work ... You have got to be in the shop, hands on, in full command of your ship. You have to build a trusting relationship with your customers. This, you can only earn over a period of time.

I'm also struck by another of Richard's characteristics, and presumably of his forebears as well. When I first met him, he said this: 'I've not been tempted to expand. I'm happy with the business being the size it is. I don't want to take over the world.' This is partly about contentment. He's passionate about Bridport, and has a feeling for geography and that deep connection to place which characterises a lot of food and drink companies. But it's also about business values. He knows that something irreplaceable would be diluted if he were incapable of seeing his customers due to managing a growing empire behind the scenes.

On the other hand, what shouldn't be read into that is a kind of romantic, dewy-eyed sense of nostalgia. Don't lose sight of the words '... it's about the here and now and planning to succeed'. And there is planning, and there is experimentation. They *have* had a second shop in recent history (to be clear, I'm talking about the last twenty years), although they took the decision to close that. And through his brother, who lives in the USA, there is a prepared frozen meat business in the States that carries the Balson name, and is perfectly adapted to the lifestyle of American families, while being based on the family sausage recipes that have been handed down from Balson father to Balson son through the ages.

In addition, Richard is fanatical about being up to date. As he writes, 'If I had said to my father forty years ago, when I started in the business, that we would be selling kangaroo, wild boar, bison and crocodile, he would have said "You're off your rocker, son."' But long-lived businesses evolve, and Richard knows this better than most. His family has been lucky to be in a timeless business – we've always eaten meat, and will do for the foreseeable future – but the fashions around it change. As but one example, for all that the Balson sausage recipe has indeed been around for generations, it now has a lower fat content than it did.

But where are my manners? I've left the startled, brain-fazed Robert Balson gawping at his far-distant descendant, half a millennium on from his entrepreneurial moment, and looking around at this well-stocked, clean environment, protected from the elements. Of course, it's imaginary, but in another sense it's also a thought experiment. I started this chapter with the word 'imagine' and humour me for a moment. Let's imagine that this feat of time travel could have happened. Other than learning that his family name and a strange version of butch-ering were to persist into the far-distant future, precisely what would Robert Balson have learned that would have done him any good in establishing his business?

I contend that he'd have learned nothing of any practical use. He'd still have to go back to his own time and do all the things that establishing his business was going to demand of him. He was going to have to work incredibly hard; create continuing relationships with suppliers; develop a large enough group of customers to keep him viable; serve them well; learn the tricks of his trade; be fair in his pricing; earn a reputation for good quality; be resilient against difficulties; stay healthy. Oh, and as we've seen, not fall behind with his rent.

It's a very big ask. And, interestingly, it's pretty much the same that is required of people in business today. Times change, the technology changes, but the fundamentals of running a sound business don't. So we'd better get Robert back to 15 September 1515. After all, he's got a dynasty to start.

5

TRUE TO PURPOSE

Claire Bodanis

PART I

Extract from Cambridge University Press Annual Report for the year ended 30 March 2034

CHAIRMAN'S INTRODUCTION

> There shall be in the University a University Press which shall be devoted to printing and publishing in the furtherance of the acquisition, advancement, conservation and dissemination of knowledge in all subjects; to the advancement of education, religion, learning and research; and to the advancement of literature and good letters.
>
> *Statute J of the University of Cambridge: The University Press*

It is 500 years since Henry VIII licensed the University of Cambridge to print and publish books, 450 since the Press's very first book, *Two Treatises of the Lord His Holie Supper*, was published, and it is a great honour to have been appointed Chairman of the Press Syndicate in this important anniversary year.

I say important not only because half a millennium of continuous existence and operation is something to be celebrated; I say important because what the Press does – what it has always done – matters enormously, never more so than in a world increasingly dominated by ignorance and fear.

Our purpose, enshrined in our Statute, is to advance learning, knowledge and research. In recent years, various extreme political, religious and ideological factors in the Middle East and elsewhere have made it ever more difficult for us to live up to that purpose. But we continue to remain true to it by standing for the tolerance, openness and embrace of knowledge that were established at our foundation. We seek knowledge. We acquire, advance, conserve and disseminate knowledge. And, in the tradition of our predecessors of the last 500 years, we will continue to do so.

With censorship now the law in many formerly open-minded Western nations, and self-censorship becoming all too common even here in Britain, Cambridge University Press stands out and must continue to stand out as a beacon of free speech and scholarly research into any and every subject worthy of study. Science, politics, religion, literature, philosophy, economics, mathematics – we are and must continue to be the leading platform for free-thinkers and rational thought the world over.

And I am humbled by the commitment and dedication of the Press's many employees who, despite the very real dangers, continue to defend and pursue our purpose robustly.

Increasing our reach in the Middle East

Our Arabic Language division (AL-CUP), which celebrated its
tenth anniversary this year, is central to this endeavour, providing
alternative sources of information, literature and authority, and
promoting the cause of liberal, modern Islam. I am particularly
heartened, therefore, to report that AL-CUP is now hard on the
heels of our largest division, Cambridge English & Education, in
terms of revenue and profit.

The growth of AL-CUP is also confirmation of the CUP strategy,
being perhaps the best example of how staying faithful to the spirit
of our purpose drives success.

If we go back a few years to the end of the last century, too
much of the Press was focused on 'printing and publishing', which
represents only one way of fulfilling our core purpose of advancing
learning and knowledge. Books and content were published in
traditional printed and digital formats, and, in its focus on the
means, the Press had begun to lose sight of the ends.

This is not surprising given that, for many centuries, the means
had indeed achieved the ends – printing and publishing were the
only way to pursue our purpose. However, in the twenty-first
century the whole notion of how to achieve the dissemination
of knowledge and the advancement of learning, and the role
of publishing within that, had to be reconsidered. As such, the
strategic review of my predecessor in 2020 was a key turning point
in the fortunes of the Press.

In focusing on the core of the purpose, the CUP leadership team at the time was encouraged to ask questions such as 'how, in today's interconnected world, can we disseminate knowledge in all subjects to people everywhere? How do we advance education, religion, learning and research when in many parts of the world people's minds are being closed through indoctrination by oppressive regimes?' Building the answers to these questions into operational and commercial decisions led to the establishment of AL-CUP in 2024.

Such thinking also led to our decision this year to expand the remit of AL-CUP into news, when the BBC's sadly underfunded World Service finally pulled out of the Middle East, leaving no independent reporting in the region. Our move has been much criticised in the media – 'brave' being perhaps the most positive reference. Commentators cited our absence of a track record in this field, and the difficulties of making journalism pay. And, indeed, it does remain to be seen how quickly AL-CUP News begins to deliver to the bottom line.

However, a business that has been in operation for 500 years has a duty to think beyond next year's balance sheet or, indeed, that of five or ten years hence. Our investment in AL-CUP News was made with an eye to our long-term future. Independent, impartial journalism goes hand in hand with the dissemination of learning: where there is no freedom for independent thinking, no tradition of broad-based education, we have no customers.

Good quality news reporting needs two things: excellent people and the right infrastructure and technology. We were fortunate to bring on board much of the World Service's team in the region, alongside a number of freelances who had been operating under the radar. And, our tech hub in Silicon Valley, another product of the aforementioned strategic review, which celebrates its thirteenth anniversary this year, is providing the technical know-how we need under the leadership of its new Chief Technology Officer. You will find a special section on AL-CUP News later in this report.

Developing Virtual Cambridge

Alongside AL-CUP, our fastest growing market is tertiary education, thanks to our VCU (Virtual Cambridge University) product. VCU enables students who cannot attend Cambridge to experience a virtual reality education, including real-time connections with staff and students, both college- and faculty-based, within Cambridge.

VCU was our tech hub's first project when the tightening of border controls in the wake of the collapse of the European Union in 2020 made it increasingly difficult – almost impossible in some cases – for the brightest students from around the world to come to study at Cambridge. Piloted, not surprisingly, with the Computer Science Department, VCU has since been rolled out across English, Modern and Mediaeval Languages, Oriental Studies, Islamic Studies, Philosophy, Mathematics, Divinity, History, Human Social & Political Sciences and Engineering. It is now offered by Christ's, Corpus Christi, Downing, Girton, Jesus, Newnham, Pembroke, Queens', St John's, Trinity and Trinity Hall. Darwin, Fitzwilliam, Gonville &

Caius and Selwyn are expected to follow in the coming year. This year, we have begun working with Natural Sciences and Medicine to develop their own bespoke VCU product which we expect to come on-stream sometime in the 2037 financial year. The practical requirements of these disciplines present more obstacles for the VCU team, not just from a technological perspective, but also from a regulatory and philosophical standpoint. However, the strong revenue stream from existing VCU products has more than delivered a return on the original investment, and will easily fund the increased R&D budget needed to reach the world's best students with these complex subjects. We are being helped enormously here by partnerships with Cambridge-trained doctors and scientists in India and China, two of our key markets, who have brought essential local colour to the development of the virtual experience – you will find more details of this project in the R&D section of this report.

The core challenge of VCU which we have had to negotiate right from the start has been how to ensure that it enhances rather than detracts from one of our core assets, the Cambridge University brand. A Cambridge University education based around the College system remains second to none, and retaining the rigour and discipline of our degrees has been fundamental to the project's success – as such we have been very careful to ensure that a VCU degree has no difference in status from a traditional degree.

Looking towards the millennium
As I write, CUP's Quincentenary Team are finalising plans for the celebrations that will run from May to October, covering a host

of events both within Cambridge and at CUP facilities around the world. We are particularly honoured that the King and Queen have accepted our invitation to the Quincentennial Banquet at the Senate House in June, preceded by a service of thanksgiving and remembrance for the lives of colleagues we have lost at the University Church, Great St Mary's. We are looking forward to bringing together many CUP colleagues from both near and far at what promises to be an event to remember in the annals of CUP.

There is no doubt that CUP faces many challenges ahead – political, ideological, commercial and practical. And that is just in the next five to ten years, let alone the next fifty, 100 or 500. What the Press will look like in any of those years I would hesitate to predict. However, I am in absolutely no doubt that, as long as our successors remain true to our purpose, CUP will come to celebrate 1,000 years of success in furthering the acquisition, advancement, conservation and dissemination of knowledge in all subjects; of advancing education, religion, learning and research; and of advancing literature and good letters to people everywhere.

© Edward Leigh

Printers checking page proofs, early twentieth century.

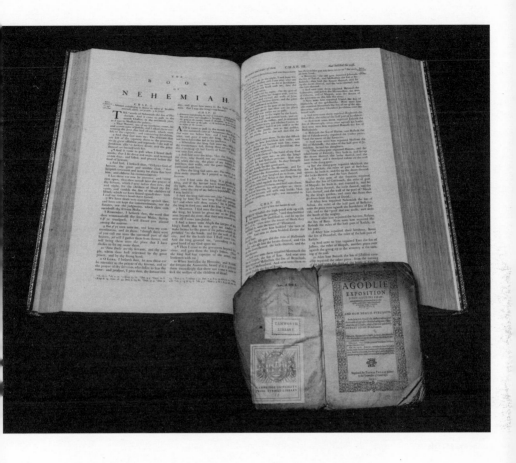

King James Bible, published by CUP in 1763, open at the Book of
Nehemiah, with one of CUP's earliest printed books, a commentary on
Nehemiah by James Pilkington, Bishop of Durham, published in 1585.

© Ramsey and Muspratt, from the Cambridgeshire Collection, Cambridge Central Library

Typesetting by hand, early twentieth century.

Modern printing on the Heidelberg Speedmaster press.

PART II
Reflections by the Author

Cambridge University Press has been there in the background of my life for many years - as a printer of exam papers during my teenage years; as a publisher of the mediaeval journals we used to fight over in the University Library because there were never enough copies to go round; as the way my friends learned English when I was living abroad. And, even when I'd left academia for good, the sight of the large CUP logo filling up the window as the London train pulled into the platform at Cambridge Station meant I could never forget it altogether. CUP was, and is, just there.

I'd never given much thought to why it was there until we started planning this book. I wasn't surprised that CUP was nearly 500 years old, though - after all, the University itself is more than 800 years old. But what did surprise me was to discover that it is a commercial enterprise that is required by the University to turn a profit. If I'd thought about it at all, I would have assumed that it was subsidised by the University to publish Cambridge academics' research papers, and had picked up English language teaching and exam papers as a natural extension of academic publishing.

Wrong in so many ways. In fact, one of the things that CUP hasn't always done is to publish some of the University's best research. In the mid-twentieth century the Press was strongly focused on the humanities, meaning that many of the University's greatest scientific discoveries were published elsewhere, something that CUP is working to change today.

And, as I looked into the Press's history I discovered that commercial success up to the late twentieth century was built largely on bibles and technology. Printing bibles for the expanding British Empire had been a highly profitable exercise, and, until the mid-twentieth century, CUP was at the forefront of printing press technology.

This success had much to do with its privileged position for many years of its existence. In its early years, CUP, along with Oxford and the King's (or Queen's) Printer, essentially had a monopoly, being the only presses allowed a licence by the monarch. After all, it's relatively easy to make money in publishing when you have an increasingly literate population and restrictions on your competitors. You could also argue that the Press has been protected from commercial reality by being part of the University. Indeed, if CUP had not been a University Department, after it lost its way commercially in the late 1960s it is possible that it could have failed – but its governing body decided to take action and give the Press a thorough overhaul rather than flogging it off to a competitor as an ordinary commercial business might have done. Every business, if it is to survive, needs to react to changes in the competitive environment.

But there is clearly more to CUP than benefiting from a legacy of monopoly (which, after all, came to an end in the mid-twentieth century) and from well-placed hands on the coat-tails of the University. On the contrary, while the reputation of the University gives kudos to the Press, the reputation of CUP around the world (today more than 90 per cent of its revenue comes from outside the UK) returns the compliment. The brand – closely associated with the University itself – is strong and one of the reasons why CUP continues to thrive. In the case of CUP there is a close relationship between brand and reputation. In fact, they are almost synonymous, which is often not the case with more recently established businesses.

And what is that reputation based on? The strongest thread throughout the Press's history is, in my view, the commitment to its purpose enshrined today in the University Statutes. But it's about the spirit rather than the letter of that purpose.

When CUP was struggling financially in the late 1960s, my reading is that it had strayed from the spirit of the purpose and become fixated on the letter - printing, traditional ideas of publishing, 'literature and letters'. And it failed to seize the enormous publishing opportunity of the University's leadership in science. Had CUP got in on the ground and made itself the publishing house of choice for scientists, it could have become the greatest scientific publisher in the world. Perhaps those who were running the Press at the time were more interested in the literary world than the scientific. People in business and in academia tend to follow their own tastes and interests - sometimes that can be a strength; often it is a weakness. Challenge can be a necessary antidote to complacency - and, who knows, with what's happening today in its academic publishing division, perhaps CUP will yet become the top scientific publisher.

The world of CUP - and publishing - is very different in 2017 from what it was in the late twentieth century. All publishers are reconsidering what publishing means, and what its business model should be, in a digital age when anyone can 'publish' content. This is a world where people increasingly expect to get information for free, and where traditional sources of authority are being questioned. CUP is certainly grappling with these questions, and there is a lively internal debate. But there is also a consistent theme - commitment to the *spirit* of the purpose: the team at CUP is fully aware that it's the spirit not the letter that matters, because sticking to the letter would soon put the Press out of business.

Coming back to the question 'how on earth did they manage it?', the resounding answer is this: by finding a successful commercial path that keeps the Press true to its purpose. It is absolutely what CUP is focused on today, and it remains a lesson to modern businesses everywhere.

6

SUMMONED BY BELLS

John Simmons

I RING. The woman at the other end of the telephone asks me, 'Which parish are you?'

This tells me much that I need to know about the Whitechapel Bell Foundry. I know that it was established in 1570 and has been making bells ever since. In fact its real history goes back to the early fifteenth century but the archives don't extend that far, and what are 150 years in this span of time?

Time. Bells and time are close family members. The bells mark the passing of time, the curfew tolls the knell of parting day and the alarm bell wakes us up so that the church bell can summon us to start the day, perhaps with a prayer.

The Whitechapel Bell Foundry seems to depend on prayer. Its owner Alan Hughes tells me that the church trades - bell founders, stonemasons, stained glass artists and many more - are united by one fact. None of them really make money. All of them are more interested in what they do than making money out of it. I imagine the Tudor poet John Skelton (as a priest he would have known such bells soon after their casting):

From casters of metals
To soakers of petals
The makers of pews
The painters of views
Masons in stone
Carvers of bone
Coming hand in hand
All eager to stand
On holy land.
But never cease to wonder
The bellman is the founder.

I ponder the word 'founder'. It is fundamental to industrial development. Of course metal casting goes back far beyond the upstart days of the Whitechapel Bell Foundry. We even define the early ages of human development by the act of casting: Iron Age, Bronze Age. It enabled civilisation to develop – and certainly war. Then, of course, we needed religion to bless those making war and peace.

Bells are associated with Christianity more than any other religion, though the world's biggest bell for ringing is said to be in Burma. This biggest bell is struck: it does not swing to ring, and the sound is so low that it hardly carries. You feel it rather than hear it. In Christianity bells were originally rung to gather a crowd to listen to the evangelist. Then from early times, when churches were built, bells were placed in towers to call the faithful, sometimes to warn of danger, at other times to lift people's hearts with the sheer joy of being alive. You sense that with the old nursery rhyme that begins:

Oranges and lemons,
Say the bells of St Clement's.

The point is that bells are part of our history and culture. The Whitechapel Bell Foundry has survived because it makes a product that is resonant in all our thinking and feeling, no matter what our religious beliefs. If the company cast more obviously industrial products it might be more profitable but less famous and less loved. (In fact, in the Second World War it made aluminium castings for the Royal Navy and did well out of it.)

Now, and for all its history, the company makes bells. It hangs bells and reconditions bells, but the problem with the business model is that its products last for centuries. There are bells all around the world, made centuries ago by the Whitechapel Bell Foundry, and they are still ringing. Events such as the Great Fire of London brought an unforeseen spike in demand. Built-in obsolescence is not a concept known in this world. The product range starts with individual church bells and carillons and extends to musical handbells. Then there are ships' bells, level-crossing warning bells, bells for clocks and music boxes, replica ambulance bells, town criers' bells, tubular bells, table bells, school bells, treble bells, alarm bells, cowbells. Not surprisingly the company's trademark (since 1583) is the sign of three bells.

Why stop at three? The nursery rhyme reminds us that churches and commerce and history have been part of the sound system. When I visit the Foundry for a public tour, an information panel tells me that the ancient bell (Robertus) of St Clement's was manufactured by the company. This also reminds me that this is part of my own history because, as a boy at St Clement Danes, the local primary school in Drury

Bells awaiting orders from on high.

Lane, I represented the school at the church's reconsecration in 1958. It had been badly bombed during the war but the big bell had survived.

You owe me five farthings,
Say the bells of St Martin's.

When I meet Alan Hughes, the current owner, and his wife Kathryn, I ask them questions about business survival. The Hughes family has been involved in the business since Alan's great-grandfather Arthur was appointed Foundry manager in 1883. Since then the business has passed down through the family, and it currently employs twenty-five people in premises that date back to 1738, with some expansion and modernisation along the way. But Alan insists the business still deals (metaphorically) in farthings. There is no prospect of becoming a big business in the future. He has read letters from his grandfather in the First World War complaining at the lack of prospects, and now he has the same tune. 'A healthy pessimism keeps us cheerful.'

People who need bells know where to find them. In the 1850s Viscount Townshend ordered three bells for his parish church in Norfolk, leaving space for five more to complete the set. In 2002 his great-great-grandson decided it was time to finish the order so the church now has eight bells made by the Whitechapel Bell Foundry. Obviously patience is a virtue but it's not always one that's accepted in business. There is a modern urgency to marketing that does not allow such a willingness to bide one's time. But time rhymes with chime.

For the Whitechapel Bell Foundry marketing is mainly about still being there. 'Everyone who needs to know knows who we are and where we are.' Its competitors have died off as the market has shrunk. Now there is only one UK competitor (in Loughborough) and few direct competitors worldwide, because the market is defined by the growth and decline of the British Empire and the Anglican Church that travelled with it. Bell-ringing became a distinctively British aspect of church-going; other branches of Christianity, other religions, just don't have the same call on bells. The very English concept of change-ringing, with a set of bells, was a musical innovation – and a useful commercial idea because it required multiple rather than individual bells. Keep ringing the changes, as we say. 'In Europe,' Mark Backhouse the factory manager tells the tour group, 'continental foundries are museums that make bells occasionally. We have a busy Foundry that's occasionally a museum.'

An interesting museum, too, with a fascinating guided tour that takes two hours. During the tour the visitor finds out about the manufacturing process which seems to have changed very little over the centuries. At the time of the Foundry's foundation in 1570 William Shakespeare was a little boy playing hopscotch and singing nursery rhymes.

When will you pay me?
Say the bells of Old Bailey.

Inevitably, finance is an issue. Whitechapel makes about one hundred bells a year, and church bells represent about three-quarters of the business. There is bell-hanging, too, almost as a consultancy service, plus the making of musical handbells. The public tours, guided by Alan or Mark, take place on Saturdays when the Foundry is not manufacturing. 'Because

Bells in differing states of casting and storage
on the floor of the Whitechapel Bell Foundry in 2016.

we don't charge for our time, we make a little money on them – that's our profit,' says Alan.

There is the question of how the business will continue in the future. The market is shrinking, but it has always been shrinking. Unless we foresee the Apocalypse arriving imminently there will remain a need for churches to commission new bells, to replace old bells that have finally expired. What about succession planning? Alan and Kathryn have two daughters, both with good jobs in business, so they are learning much of what is needed. 'But this is the fourth generation,' says Alan, 'and most businesses change after four generations. I think that change of ownership is a good thing. It renews a business; that has been part of the history of this company, it has changed ownership. The mistake my father made was to take me here straight from school. I would have been better at what I do if I'd gone somewhere else first.'

> When I grow rich,
> Say the bells of Shoreditch.

Surely these days you need technology to grow rich? You need to come up with a brilliant idea that uses technology? Then, like Bill Gates and Mark Zuckerberg, you can make so much money that you have to give it away. The alternative approach, chosen by the Foundry, is to stick to your centuries-old craft and make just enough to survive. You become rich in your own estimation of life and that, surely, is beyond financial value. 'We have been fortunate, privileged, to meet all these people. Queens and archbishops, prime ministers and presidents, whom we meet and it seems we are on equal terms because we don't fit into a particular social box, we do something that people like to be associated with.' There is the new royalty, the A-grade celebrities, who drop into the premises out of interest and to place an order: Jeremy Paxman, Clive Anderson, Damon Albarn, Dan Snow, Suggs, Danny Boyle. And not forgetting Mrs Windsor, as the paperwork states, whose payments come from the Privy. Unfortunately you don't gain wealth by association.

There is far more truth in the old saying 'where there's muck there's brass'. Here is a manufacturing process that takes base metals and creates a golden tone. A bell is made – and they are all made to order, as one-offs – by pouring molten metal into a bell-shaped space within a mould. The mould uses loam – a mixture of sand, clay, horse manure, goat's hair and water – applied by hand. It's a craft activity that makes you wonder: how did they first stumble on this way of doing things? But in essence the manufacturing process is the same as that carried out by monks in medieval monasteries, using an alloy that is 77 per cent copper and 23 per cent tin. When stocks of certain materials are running low, the Foundry sends some of its people out into the country areas around London on a 'dung run'.

Some new technology is used but the basic craft remains the same. Computers make some office tasks easier – for example, updating estimates when a customer resurfaces many years after a first enquiry. But the bespoke nature of the business means that a computerised assembly line would never repay the investment, particularly when many bells require inscriptions or decorations. 'In the 1970s we tried to standardise, but it didn't work. Every church needed its own quirks.' A high level of craft skills is needed, and this kind of manufacturing takes time – and, it is true, time is money. Perhaps we need to value time much more than we do.

When will that be?
Say the bells of Stepney.

Time is also infinitely stretchable. I get the sense that the company's obsession with marking the passing of time has helped to make it as special as it is. It makes you realise that deadlines are important but you have to take a broad view, look at things changing over the long run. Which leads to a rather phlegmatic approach to customer service. It might be true that the customer is always right, so you have to listen and adapt – but not necessarily to jump right away.

Survival has been helped by a somewhat sceptical attitude to life and customers. The company motto (displayed around the factory, pointed out in the joinery with some pride) is: 'Nothing is impossible for the man who doesn't have to do it himself'. You can imagine them chuckling at that one behind the customer's back after he placed an order; and then the carpenter sighing when his boss passed the order on for making. But the reality is that they can make things that seem impossible to make, because they have such a high level of skills and experience. 'If someone asks "Could you?" we listen. If someone else asks the same question soon after, we make sure we can do it.' Alan Hughes believes it is an ability to make and adapt to anything that has helped the company survive.

This flexibility applies to selling and marketing even if the company claims its marketing is invisible. Interviews are not easily given because the benefits are not always apparent: the market is not for expanding. But word of mouth, the most ancient and the most modern form of marketing, seems to come naturally. Cooperation was granted readily when the radio soap opera *The Archers* approached them. The reward was a broadcast storyline including a conversation in which Shula talks about 'that nice Mr Hughes from Whitechapel'. Which was amusing, but it became better when the invoice for a bell's manufacture, provided for the sake of reality, was read out and discussed as part of the script.

Mr Hughes from Whitechapel is not a man to stick to his own parish. He gets out and about, travelling the world with his iPad to take and fulfil orders. He benefits, no doubt, from Britain's history, perhaps one of the last areas of commerce to feel the residual effects of the colonial past. One third of the Foundry's production is exported to countries like Australia, New Zealand, Canada and Australia. The USA is a big export market and I meet Mr Hughes soon after he returns on business from Rochester, New York. On other trips he has been invited into the White House, and, of course, the Liberty Bell in Philadelphia was made in Whitechapel. Now it is one of the USA's most significant historical artefacts, its story even enriched by the fact that it is cracked, having been damaged on the sea voyage. The offer to remake it was declined because it had become such a powerful symbol.

Alan Hughes has a good stock of stories that are worth more than the company's raw materials. He tells, with a sense of wonder, how he took a phone call from a gentleman in the town of Liberty, Kentucky. Rather sheepishly the man asked about the company: 'Did you make the Liberty Bell?'

'Yes, we did.'

'Would it be possible to make a replica?'

'Of course.'

'How do I order?'

It turned out that the man on the phone was the Mayor of Liberty. He was so pleased to be ordering a bell from the same

The Liberty Bell was ordered in 1751 by Pennsylvania from the Whitechapel Bell Foundry. The bell was shipped across the Atlantic but declared 'cracked' on arrival. The bell became a powerful symbol associated with the Declaration of Independence and then the abolitionist movement. It now has its own visitor centre in Philadelphia.

company at the same address as the original manufacturers that he ordered and paid for it himself.

A second story follows, a recent example of a couple seeking out the company. An American couple, living on the shores of the Great Lakes, decided to sail their ocean-going yacht across the Atlantic. They arrived in London, moored the yacht in St Katharine Docks, then walked the short distance to Whitechapel. Having visited the Foundry, having been transported by the experience, they decided that the mission was accomplished, returned to their yacht and sailed away – they wanted to see nothing else in Britain.

Will they return?

Will customers keep coming?

I do not know,
Says the great bell of Bow.

The reason why the Foundry is where it is goes back into history. Location is everything, or at least it was. The definition of a Cockney, a native Londoner, is someone born within hearing distance of Bow Bell. Originally the Foundry that made Bow Bell was on the eastern edge of London with green fields for neighbours: the prevailing wind could take the smells of manufacturing away from the city's population. More importantly, in terms of the economics of the business, the location meant that transport was made easy. With such heavy products, transport by river, sea and canal was vital. In more recent times, London's advantage as a transport hub – for road, rail, air – has been essential for the business's survival. The basics of history, reputation and location mean that the business survives and, in one sense, thrives. It is certainly London's oldest manufacturer and it can still teach modern manufacturers much, as long as they set aside those truisms of the business world.

Conventional business books might tell you that a company needs to:

- Grow or go out of business
- Innovate or die
- Diversify the product range and keep doing it
- Bring in new technology or else.

Here, by contrast, is a company that does what it has always done. It makes bells. There is no market to expand, but people who need bells made, hung or repaired still find the company. The manufacturing process has hardly changed in 500 years, depending still on traditional craft skills and organic materials. Today it is generally reckoned by those who know to be the world's best in its field.

What creates perfection? Perhaps the realisation that, actually, no such thing is possible but what matters is the constant striving to do your best, and to do what you do supremely well, but with the awareness that you can do the next job even better. 'Ring the bells,' sings Leonard Cohen in his song 'Anthem' and then gives the reason for that celebration as, 'for there's a crack, a crack in everything, that's how the light gets in.' The Liberty Bell might stand as a symbol of that.

Businesses need to take the patient long view but increasingly they take the impatient short-term view. New businesses could look over the nearest hedge fund to see green fields beyond, and see those places, as the Whitechapel founders did, as opportunities to serve a deeper need. These could be opportunities to do something that enhances the quality of life, that

Time to ring the changes. Bells stored in the foundry's yard,
waiting to be moved to new ownership.

meets a human and spiritual need not just a financial one, that gives us all a reason to celebrate.

To ring the bells

But bells can crack. At the end of 2016 it was announced that Alan Hughes was selling the company (the fourth generation, as he had warned). First reports that the company was disappearing were not correct, but it will be sold and the aim is to move to new premises under new ownership. This latest twist does not contradict but reinforces the messages of its nearly 500-year history. If it survives, in a new form, it will prove its adaptability. If not, it will have lost its useful and meaningful purpose. Whatever happens, its products will continue to gladden hearts, probably for centuries to come.

7

''TIS THE CASK, NOT THE COFFER, THAT HOLDS THE TRUE WEALTH'

Neil Baker

'I T'S LUCK. IT'S LUCK,' repeats Simon Berry, chairman
of Berry Bros. & Rudd, Britain's oldest wine and spirit
merchant. We're sitting in his snug office, known
simply as The Parlour, drinking tea from china cups. Outside,
it's a freezing London morning. In here, the gas fire emits a
comforting hiss. There's no computer, no electronic devices at
all. Portraits of family members, past and present, fill the walls.
A loose thread hangs from the stitching of Simon's black shoes.
A clock ticks.

Simon turns up the fire and warms to his theme: how the
family firm owned by Berrys and Rudds that he now leads has
remained in business since 1698, when a woman remembered
only as the Widow Bourne started selling groceries from a shop
at 3 St James's Street.

It was good luck, he says, that almost as soon as the business opened its doors, St James's Palace, just across the street,
became the principal residence of the British monarchy. It was
good luck, too, that nobody interrupted future president of
France Napoleon III when he used the dark cellars at St James's
Street to hold secret meetings during his years of political exile
in London. It was good luck that America banned the import

and sale of alcohol, because Berry Bros. & Rudd started sending spirits to the Bahamas, which led to the invention of Cutty Sark Scotch whisky, which underpinned the firm's profits for years. It was good luck the firm started selling wines and spirits in airport duty-free shops just as the middle-class boom hit China and Asia. And it was good luck that in 1994, almost 300 years after its founding, the firm stumbled onto the idea of selling on the internet, becoming an ecommerce pioneer. 'There's also the luck,' he continues, 'of making sure the best people in the two families join the firm, while the worst are kept as far away as possible!'

So, yes, luck, luck, luck. But the luck had been bad as well as good. Anthony Berry, Simon's father, was desperate to work in the wine trade. 'But his father, my grandfather, told him that he would be an architect instead,' says Simon. 'Of course, he couldn't even build with Lego. But they gave him the drawing desk and told him to get on with it.' Then the Second World War intervened. Anthony's elder brother, George, was expected to run the firm for a generation. He died while leading a charge against the enemy in North Africa. Brian Rudd was the next family member in line. He was killed in action in Italy. So Anthony ended up running the business after all, and he did a remarkably good job of it. The firm grew under his command and by 2015 was selling around 5,000 wines and spirits; had offices in Japan, Singapore and Hong Kong, as well as London; ran its own wine school; and had turnover of £142m.

But can a business really survive – let alone thrive – for over 300 years on luck alone? I don't think so. And I'm sure Simon doesn't either. Just look at the crucial decision the family took twenty years ago to bring in outside managers. That was a result of honest self-reflection and sound business planning, not fortunate timing. But, as we sit chatting in his snug parlour, I begin to wonder if there's a reason why he likes to talk so much about luck and fate and the serendipitous twists and turns that have kept his business moving forwards for so long. When it's time to leave, and I step out into the sunny Mayfair morning, the answer seems obvious: Simon is a born storyteller.

One of the stories he tells is of teenage rebellion.

Today he is the oldest family member working in the business full time. I ask him if he can remember a moment, as a young man, when he knew that he wouldn't be 'pruned from the tree', as he puts it, like his father had been – before the family told young Anthony to give up the architectural career they had foisted upon him, to put down his set square and to pick up the baton that had slipped from his dying brother's grasp in North Africa. Can Simon remember the moment when he knew his future was to work for the firm, when he felt fate tap *him* on the shoulder? 'No,' he says.

'But I can remember the time I thought I never would work here,' he continues. 'I was nineteen when I escaped. It was an odd form of teenage rebellion, but that's effectively what it was. I'd been here for about a year, I was still living with my parents, and I went back home and said "I'm going to stop working here." It was as if I'd said to my father "I'm going to go and live on Mars." He just couldn't process it; wouldn't process it. My mother said, "Are you on drugs?" Then I left.'

Simon's dream was to run away and become a writer. 'At the time I had a godmother who was in publishing,' he says. 'I wrote a book and sent it to her. She'd been nice enough to read it, and took me out to lunch. I was expecting her to say fine we'll publish it and sell the film rights next week.' Instead, she told

After 319 years of profitable business, Berry Bros. & Rudd opened its second London shop in 2017. The new premises on Pall Mall are better suited to the needs of modern retail, the company says. But the old St James's Street shop is just around the corner, and a private passageway connects the two. The link with the past is unbroken.

him it was awful. Her advice was to write radio plays, because there were two on the BBC each day - somebody had to write them. 'I thought that was a good idea. But because I was a teenager and knew everything, I thought radio plays would be too easy so decided to get into the film industry. I discovered it was full of the biggest load of dickheads I'd ever met.'

The 'pipe dream', as Simon calls it, had exploded. He came back to the family firm. 'In a sense, my rebellion had been a failure,' he concedes.

But any sense of failure was fringed with something more positive. In his time away from the firm, Simon had seen it in a different light. 'There was a realisation that I could make a difference here,' he says. 'There was something I could do, if I carved out my own niche. I was never going to be a Master of Wine. I think I also knew I'd never be the world's greatest businessman; that wasn't my ambition. But I'd realised that a company like this isn't just about commerce, and it isn't just about wine. Here was something that had been around for almost three hundred years. The fascination was, what happens next? My ambition was to carry on the story, and to tell the story. That's what brought me back, the story.'

And having told the story of his own rebellion, he says perhaps it wasn't the idea of working in the family firm that he was rejecting all those years ago, just the assumption that he would simply accept this fate. 'I didn't want my life to be pigeonholed by something somebody three hundred years before had decided to do,' he says. 'I've always been slightly rebelling against it ever since, which is why I appreciate rebels. I'm trying to encourage my nephew, Geordie, to be one.' At his suggestion, a month later, I go to meet Geordie Willis.

Up many twisting staircases to the chilly boardroom. Ten chairs around the table. Above the empty fireplace, a stone polar bear and two Queen's Awards for Industry, for 1971 and 1981. On the walls, paintings of the Berry Bros. & Rudd board in session; John Rudd in oils. And on the other side of the table, Geordie – bearded, suave, Instagram-savvy creative director and, at thirty-three, the youngest Berry or Rudd currently working in the business.

'I never expected to be in the wine trade,' he begins, when I ask him to tell me his story. 'I grew up in Scotland so was quite far removed from the business on a day-to-day basis. My parents weren't part of it. And while I was aware of it, I wasn't running around the cellars as a toddler.' Instead, Geordie wanted to work in magazines. After university – where he read English – he landed a job in London. The pay was so bad that he could only afford to get the bus either to or from work, not both. 'So I started working here for pocket money – below ground, in the cellars. I was in jeans and t-shirt, shifting boxes and putting in some hard graft for three years. I found myself learning a fair bit, not through tasting wine, but through picking up bottles and moving them around.'

He enjoyed the business so left the magazine world and became a full-time employee. 'One day, after about a year and a half, just as I was thinking everything was going well, I got called upstairs by the new chairman (Uncle Simon). That didn't happen too often. As I'd been working hard, I assumed it was probably about a promotion. He said, "When are you leaving?" I said, well I thought that was the joy of a family business – that one didn't have to leave. And he said you obviously haven't read your contract very carefully.'

In the small print was a rule that said any family member

joining the business had to work somewhere else for at least two years. Geordie thought it didn't apply to him, because he'd done his time in the magazine trade. He was wrong. 'This was a rule they brought in with my generation, inspired by a course Simon had done at Harvard. Surprisingly, now I do the maths, I wonder if that might have been his first official act as chairman: getting rid of me. In fact, thinking back now, working in magazines was probably Simon's suggestion too. You know, it's starting to sound like he doesn't want me to work here!'

So, like his uncle many years before, Geordie found himself cut off from the family firm. Whereas Simon pursued the bohemian life of the penniless writer – for a while at least – Geordie became a brand and design consultant. 'I worked in Chelsea,' he says. 'In terms of being thrown into the wilderness, it was OK.'

For Geordie, life outside Berry Bros. & Rudd was a great success – to the point where he didn't expect to come back. But travelling through Asia, he dropped into the firm's Hong Kong office for a drink with a friend. They talked about plans to expand in the region. As with his uncle before him, the storytelling potential of Berry Bros. & Rudd lured him back. After four years working on its marketing in Asia, Geordie returned to London as brand director.

'Immediately I started on a ... well, a rebranding sounds a little aggressive. It was really more of an archaeology project,' he explains. 'If you look at what makes us interesting in the modern world, it's our ability to tell compelling stories as much as anything else. I'm a firm believer, and I push for this more and more, that brands must create and tell their own stories. So we were going back into the archives, rediscovering stories that were hidden away in drawers.'

Geordie is proud of the firm's heritage, but he wanted to find a different way to tell its story. 'We went through a horrible period a few years ago where we kept making brochures with pictures of maybe an elderly gentleman holding up a bottle to a younger gentleman; that sort of "laying down wine for the future" idea. It's so bloody awful, just because it was false. The right intentions, but with no integrity. Twenty years ago our customer was a pinstriped male of a certain age, schooled in a certain place, and with a certain accent. That simply isn't the case any more. Our audience has changed dramatically.'

As a merchant, the firm has always seen itself as the link between the people who drink wine and those who make it. In a market where consumers now value provenance, something less industrial, Geordie wants to spend more time telling the stories of those makers. 'If something is mass-produced and machine-made, it doesn't have the compelling story of a small winemaker on the north coast of Sicily who is making a garage wine and has mud permanently under his fingernails and a young son and daughter who he's hoping will become the next generation of winemakers.' Geordie enjoys meeting these people and taking their photos. 'We never tell them that we want a photo beforehand, so they can't get dressed up or put a tie on. And if they ever have their children around, I always ask if they can do a portrait together.'

Telling the stories of the 400 winemakers the firm works with, and doing it in an authentic way, is not just good marketing. Geordie calls it as a responsibility. He hopes that the photos he takes and commissions will build into a valuable archive of winemakers, part of his legacy. 'I think the families we work with are as important as our family here in the firm,' he says.

Inside the new shop on Pall Mall. Staves from 100-year-old
French wine barrels line the ceiling. A bottle costs from £10
upwards, and upwards, and upwards...

As our conversation draws to a close, I ask Geordie whether his passion for telling authentic brand stories is from the same itch that his uncle tried to scratch by writing novels: is there something in the blood? 'So, Simon is a thwarted novelist,' he says, seemingly surprised – and intrigued – by the revelation of these literary ambitions in an uncle he calls his 'father in London'. 'Luckily, he's never asked me to read anything,' he says. 'We're always very honest with each other!' I tell Geordie the story of his uncle's rejection of the firm, and ask if he has a rebellion story of his own. Nothing comes to mind, or nothing that he wants to share. I don't tell Geordie that his uncle would like him to become more of a rebel.

Anthony Berry, father to Simon, grandfather to Geordie, would-be architect, died a few years ago, aged ninety-four. For seventy-five years he kept a diary in which he wrote down the name of every single wine he drank. It's because of these diaries that Simon can name the first glass of wine he ever drank – a Beaujolais, on Christmas Day, when he was eight years old. Simon has thought about publishing the diaries. 'Sadly, Father didn't write any long, expansive tasting notes. He'd just write things like "very good of its type".'

But, like his son and nephew after him, Anthony seems to have taken words – *stories* – very seriously. Before he died, he told the family to carve on his gravestone eleven words that had been a moral compass in his life – business as well as personal, as if the two could ever be disentangled in a family firm. They are the refrain from 'The Vintners' Song', which is sung with table-thumping gusto at the end of every banquet given by London's Worshipful Company of Vintners: "tis the cask, not the coffer, that holds the true wealth'.

It's a line that says this business - like life itself - is about something more than money. Simon and Geordie communicate that special 'something' by telling stories. Listening to Simon talk about the firm, I think he sees it not so much as a business but as a living story, a grand unfolding narrative. Like every great storyteller, he knows that a great tale is about people facing challenges, responding to whatever luck - good and bad - throws at them: from a brave widow opening a shop by herself 300 years ago to a son returning from professional exile to rescue his family from the tragedy of war.

I ask Simon what happened to the drawing desk that the family bought for his father, the one he would have used through his years as a trainee architect, if fate hadn't intervened. It's in the St James's Street shop, on the left as you step over the threshold, into the world of the firm. When I return to see Geordie, he shows it to me and reveals his plan to embed a digital storytelling screen in its wooden top - a plan he hasn't told Simon about yet. It sounds like an idea Anthony would have liked. Earlier, I'd asked Geordie if he ever got bored telling the old family stories to curious visitors. 'My grandfather used to say, "If you spend the whole time looking over your shoulder at the past, you will bump into the future" … But one of the responsibilities of us as the family is to make sure that the stories continue to be told. When my grandfather died, I know that a lot of stories went with him. There was something he often wrote, and reminded me of: the refrain from "The Vintner's Song" …' Ah, yes, those words again. The cask and the coffer. I ask Geordie if those words mean something special to him, too. He smiles, and I think his answer combines a bit of everything that has helped Berry Bros. & Rudd to prosper for so long - a clear sense of tradition and values, a respect for

The old shop at 3 St James's Street is now used mainly for welcoming customers. But what could be more important than that?

the power of story and a rebellious streak: 'Just after my grandfather died, I had those words, in his own handwriting, tattooed
on my ribs.'

8

THE BRUSH, THE MALLET, THE CHISEL, THE LETTER

Richard Pelletier

'John Stevens, Stone Cutter Takes this method to inform the public and his former employers in particular THAT he carries on the stone-cutters business at his shop the North end of Thames Street where any persons may be supplied with tombstones, gravestones, hearths, and printers press stones, and where every kind of work in stone is performed in the neatest and most elegant manner.'

Newport Mercury, 27 October 1781

29 Thames Street, Newport, Rhode Island

LATE AFTERNOON. A WARM SEPTEMBER DAY. Autumn light drifts down through the windows and skylights of Nicholas Benson's stone-carving shop on Thames Street in Newport, Rhode Island. High on the wall, a likeness of Nick's grandfather. He is John Howard Benson, whose creative fires stoke this place like the light of an endless sun. Nick Benson is at his workbench. Overhead on a wooden shelf, a row of mallets and wood planes, smoothed and worn, register the yawn of time, gathering dust.

The space is intimate, glorious. Thick, exposed, load-bearing beams; mallets and chisels and wood planes and ropes. Small blocks of stone carved with the letter R. ('I'm a big fan of the letter R,' says Nick. 'It incorporates all the strokes in the alphabet and it is a gorgeous form, but the Trajan School B is enough to stop my heart.') Shelves and drawers and walls are lovingly filled with old tools, drawings and sketches, letters and photographs, books and letterforms. There are thick slabs of granite, marble and slate. It's the studio of an artist of the Old World, sumptuous and magical, a visual feast. All that light. A sense of order.

In the glare of a simple desk lamp, Paul Russo carves a honed granite headstone that leans on a large wooden easel. A twenty-plus-years stone-carver, he's Nick's main man. Russo has just finished a line drawing of a sailing boat and now comes the world's shortest biography – name, date of arrival, date of departure. The going is slow; it will take him two weeks to finish. It's slow because granite is the hardest stone there is. And because this is how they do it here. (Cost of the headstone Paul is working on: $5,000.00. A commercial headstone shop would do the same in two hours for $1,800.00.) To watch for a minute is to know two things. A hand-carved headstone is a sensitive, lasting and loving tribute. And it is fierce, hard, painstaking work. 'My hands are fine,' Russo says, 'it's my elbows. I have tendinitis.'

'I have carpal tunnel,' says Nick. 'I have bad legs and my knees are killing me.'

The pace in the workshop tends towards a normal eight-hour working day. On large, site-specific projects (for which the Shop is renowned) it's different. 'On those we're going fast,' says Nick, 'putting in nine- and ten-hour days. It's brutal.'

Photograph by Michael A. Dunn, Office of the Architect of the Capitol

Nicholas W. Benson carves the Pledge of Allegiance to the United States of America into the wall of the Capitol Visitors' Centre, Washington DC.

As chisel meets granite, a rapid fire, metallic 'tenk' sound fills the workshop. Tenk, tenk, tenk, tenk, tenk. Tenk, tenk. Tenk, tenk, tenk. Memorialising the dead in granite has a music and rhythm to it, a syncopation that repeats until it doesn't. John Cage, are you listening?

Between the Shop's first, somewhat crude scratchings from the early days of the eighteenth century, and the elegant letters that Russo carves today, stand two families. The Stevens family came first. Then came the Bensons, of whom Nicholas Waite Benson is the latest. Which means that the John Stevens Shop has survived six generations of one family and three generations of another.

How Did it Begin?
The story begins in Oxfordshire, with John Stevens, a stonemason who left home in England for America and landed in Boston in 1698. We know that in Boston John met a woman named Marcy and married her. Their firstborn was a boy, John the second. For reasons unknown, the family travelled south, by sea, to Newport, Rhode Island. There, in 1705, in his mid-fifties, amidst the cobblestone streets, he established the John Stevens Shop. Principal activity: masonry. Gravestone inscriptions – of which, it appears, he knew not one single thing – quickly after.

Did he ever let himself dream? Say it was a cold, late night on Thames Street in his first year in business. Say John Stevens whispered, 'Marcy, I've got a good feeling. I think the Shop can be something.' Exhausted by her long, hard days, Marcy had fallen fast asleep.

Newport and Stevens were made for one another. The town was on a roll, artisans were in demand. His home in the New World was itself born of an odyssey. In 1639, the eight original founders of Newport fled a political kerfuffle in Portsmouth, Rhode Island, ten miles to the north. By the time Stevens got to town, there was plenty of masonry work. It didn't hurt that the colonies had a high mortality rate. There would be no shortage of customers. Stone carving has been going on more or less uninterrupted on Thames Street ever since. At the time of writing, the Shop is now 310 years old – the oldest company continually doing business in the United States.

Aside from the on-again, off-again gravestone work, the early generations of Stevenses stayed afloat on the strength of their skill as masons. They built fireplaces and chimneys; foundations for houses; they stoned cellars, they did plasterwork. They set pots on ships in a town that was thick with them. For a while, shoemaking and repair showed up in the account books – and then disappeared. They kept the lamps lit.

In both the Stevens and Benson eras, the Shop has shown a surprising knack for making relationships. They found customers, friends, kindred spirits, patrons and influential supporters among prominent Newport residents and beyond. In colonial Newport, some of the Shop's better-known customers come straight out of the history books: Coddington, Slocum, Cranston, Collins, Carr and others. In the Benson era, the names emerged from the upper strata of American (and European) art, business, letters and philanthropy. Paul and Bunny Mellon, J. Carter Brown, Charles Reiskamp, Peter Gomes, Lincoln Kirstein, Maya Lin, Edward Catich, Hermann Zapf.

John Stevens' first headstones were not much more than a scratching on the surface of the stone. Some survive in the Common Burying Ground in Newport to this day. The very first headstone recorded in the account books was for 'Major William Wanton, £ 1-10-0 to a pair of gravestones for your son'.

Only a trained eye could have seen what those rough early efforts foretold. John Stevens, it turned out, had an instinctual sense of design and in ten years he mastered the chisel. His progeny were even better. John the second, his brother William and John the third (whose advertisement is at top) were each gifted and distinctive artists.

Looking back, the Benson family were great admirers. Several hundred years after the fact, John Howard Benson wrote, 'John Stevens II and his brother William, executed particularly fine carved lower-case letters. John Stevens' grandson, John Stevens III, was especially good at low relief, ornamental carving and portraits. Their technique was instinctual, formed by a strong, innate sense of design.' Nick Benson has said, 'The Stevens letters evolved solely through the use of the mallet and chisel. They did not use brushes [as he does today] to lay out the letters they carved. And over fifty-odd years of evolution, this lower-case form was refined to a point of exceptional beauty.' The brush – an ancient Roman technique for laying out letters to be chiselled – came to the Shop much later.

Tomb of the Children of Sextus Pompeius Justus, Via Appia Antica, Rome

Nick Benson made his pilgrimage by mountain bike. 'I rode out first thing in the morning. The Appia Antica is ridiculously beautiful. It's all the original two-thousand-year-old cobblestones. You're cruising along and there it is, the Sextus. I had an absolutely religious experience.' During the Pax Romana, he tells me, came a massive boom in new buildings in marble. With it came inscriptions. 'There was a group that got especially good,' he says. 'They invented it. And took it to this insane level.'

Photograph by Richard Pelletier

Nicholas Benson at work at The John Stevens Shop, Newport, R.I.

Photograph by Nicholas W. Benson

Tomb of the children of Sextus Pompeius, Via Appia Antica, Rome.

The Trajan School and the brush technique they used to carve their letters gained worldwide attention in the twentieth century through Father Edward Catich. He was a former Chicago sign writer-turned-artist, stone-carver, calligrapher, educator and Catholic priest. His work on Trajan's Column in Rome finally helped crack the code as to how these magnificent letters were made. (Although Catich gained widespread admiration and acceptance for his work, he has his detractors.) 'I am convinced that the carver who did the work on Trajan's Column,' said Nick, 'was not the carver who did the work on the Sextus. But both inscriptions were lettered by the same person. It's the same group of lettering artists and carvers.' For Catich, the Trajan is the ideal Roman capital letter. For Nick, it's the Sextus that brings him to tears. 'See this "B"?' he asks, as he turns the pages of *The Eternal Letter: Two Millennia of the Classical Roman Capital*, by Paul Shaw. 'The emphasis on the stroke coming off the top of the bottom bowl is much more heavy than the brush would allow for. And there's a stylistic affectation in the execution of it that's particular to that group. It's extremely beautiful. You see it and you go, "Oh, my God." It has that kind of effect on me.'

Years before Nick Benson ever took up a chisel, Edward Catich introduced the brush Roman technique to a kindred spirit. He was also a trained artist, educator, calligrapher, stone-carver and scholar of the letterform. A man, it turned out, who had already found his way to the brush. His name was John Howard Benson, Nick's grandfather.

'Letters Exist to Serve Men' – John Howard Benson
The Shop's late nineteenth- and early twentieth-century work was good enough, but not much more than that. The verve and

artistic flair of the Stevens' early work was gone. In the waning years of the Stevens era, Philip Stevens, son of John the third, ran the business until 1866. Then came two of his sons, Lysander and Philip. A brother-in-law, Edwin Burdock, stepped in at the end. For a time it operated as P. Stevens and Sons. By the late twenties, it was the kind of shop that a stone-carver might lease to work on a commission. Nick describes it as a kind of men's club. The doors were open but the Shop was adrift.

Then Mrs Stanley Hughes of Newport died. She was the wife of Rev. Stanley C. Hughes of Trinity Church. The Reverend wanted a headstone to stand with the beautiful slate stones in Trinity churchyard. He wanted a headstone that would matter. He wanted *sculpture*. It was 1926.

John Howard Benson was then twenty-five years old. He was born and raised in Newport. As a young man he'd gone to New York City to study printmaking and sculpture (among other disciplines) at the National Academy of Design and the Art Students League. Early on, he'd become deeply interested in gravestones through family visits to the Common Burying Ground in Newport. In *The History of the John Stevens Shop*, his wife, Esther Fisher Benson, wrote about her husband's obsessions. 'He wrote articles on the relation of our New England headstones to their Greek and Roman prototypes. Epigraphy in its entire history, as well as lettering of every kind was his permanent occupation.' The man had arrived at his moment. The Hughes headstone was his. He took a lease on the Shop for a year and then bought it with the help of a friend, Arthur Graham Carey.

Did John Howard Benson ever let himself dream? Say that on a cold winter's night, after he'd bought the Shop, the artist leaned over to his wife and whispered, 'The Shop. I can

Edwin Burke, the last of the Stevens family, stands in the doorway
of The John Stevens Shop, Newport, R.I. *circa* 1900.

do something with it.' If we know anything of Esther Fisher Benson, she was wide awake and said, 'I believe in thee, John.'

In spite of who he was and all he knew, John Howard Benson had no formal training in lettering and had a lot to learn. Where was the best slate and how to get it to Newport? How do you shape and surface the stones? Set them on their foundations? Find skilled help? In terms of both stone carving and running a business, he was self-taught. Nick Benson said that when his grandfather got interested in the business, the shop was like most other monument shops in America: a little older and on its last legs. Being an artist, he threw all of the monumental trends and techniques of the early twentieth century out of the window and looked to the colonial work (early Stevens included) for inspiration. Because of his talent and connections, the Shop landed some very good commissions. He turned the Shop into a conduit for the Arts and Crafts Movement, of which he was a part.

In his day he established the Shop as an internationally recognised centre for stone inscriptions. He wrote two books on letters and calligraphy, *The Elements of Lettering* with the aforementioned Carey and *The First Writing Book*, a translation of *Arrighi's Operina*. After his initial eighteenth-century approach to lettering, he moved towards classical Roman capitals.

John Howard Benson attracted all sorts of interesting characters and many of them would become important to the Shop's extraordinary reach and survival. With his arrival on the scene came this new and completely astonishing ascent. As in the beginning, so it shall be again. Three generations, father, son, grandson. All three men would become internationally renowned calligraphers and stone-carvers. John Howard, and his son, John Everett, who started cutting stone at the age of fifteen and later went to the Rhode Island School of Design. And John Everett's son, Nick, who also started cutting stone at fifteen and who studied design in Basel, Switzerland. After Nick sent his request for an application to attend, he received a reply that in effect said, 'We've designed a course of study specifically for you. We know your work and your father's work. We've been waiting.'

John Everett said this about his father: 'He managed to create a really interesting life for himself.' Interesting and far too short. John Howard Benson succumbed to a heart condition and died young, at fifty-five, in 1956.

In the period after his death, Esther Fisher Benson kept things going with the help of Arthur Graham Carey, the Shop's early investor and family friend. They managed until 1961, when John Everett, then in his early twenties, stepped in and took over the Shop from his mother.

Sacred Undertakings

Say 'grassy knoll' and 'book depository' and you need no other words. After the assassination of John F. Kennedy in Dallas on 22 November 1963, the nation turned its lonely eyes to 29 Thames Street. The commission for the JFK Memorial at Arlington National Cemetery - almost a sacred undertaking - fell to twenty-five-year-old John Everett Benson. The job came into the Shop through an old connection of his father's. It would change everything. In the coming years, one high-profile commission followed another. Individually and together, John Everett Benson and Nicholas Waite Benson (who won the MacArthur 'Genius Grant' in 2010) have designed letterforms - and carved inscriptions - for an extraordinary array of public buildings and memorials. There's the JFK Memorial, the Roosevelt Memorial and the National Gallery of Art in Washington, DC, the Civil Rights Memorial in Montgomery, Alabama (with Maya Lin), the Dallas Museum of Art, the Art Institute of Chicago, the WWII Memorial on the Mall in DC, the MLK Memorial in Washington, DC, Four Freedoms Park in New York – the list and the work stretches on. 'No one else really does what we do,' said Nick, who took over from his father in 1993. By which he means the marriage of original letterform design and the stone-carving skill that makes epigraph into sculpture.

Nick is a lean, strong man and he was still vibrating with energy deep into a Thursday afternoon. The chisels had gone quiet. As he talked, there was more than a tinge of gratitude and wonder in his voice. As both steward and actor in this story, he relishes every act, scene and thread. 'This is only as good as whoever is in the driver's seat. My dad and I both talk about this. If you don't have enough interest and you're not driven by the potential of all of this, tapping into its history, then really the product is going to be soulless.'

To the question of what his customers were buying from him, he said, 'This is interesting. In all of the typographic standard that's been developed through print and now through the digital age, there's such a taint of the mechanical. In business, that's what people want. A clean, no-nonsense message.' Then he spoke about the devastating loss of a close personal friend. 'He was the other half of me,' he said. As he lettered his friend's name, date of arrival and his date of departure in preparation for a headstone, that's when he knew. 'When people have lost a loved one, they want to bring all of the humanity, all the memory from the person they lost. And this is the place that resonates most. We're taking all this time and it's all done by hand. There's all this loving care we put into it. Until it happened to me, it was brass tacks of the skill, the legacy stuff, the business. This was very heavy.'

God's Little Acre, Newport, R.I.
Just up on Thames Street is Newport's Common Burying Ground. It's a block or two east from where the first slave ships arrived in 1696. In a section called God's Little Acre – also known as the Colonial African Burial Ground – is a headstone with a strikingly lively, artistic style. Cherub's head, wings, deeply cut leaves. It looks like the work of John Stevens the second, or the third. But the artist was Zingo Stevens, an African slave, who signed his work in memory of his deceased brother. This stone is recognised as one of the first pieces of art signed by an African in the Americas. Zingo Stevens' recently discovered prayer book is now at the Beinecke Library at Yale University. Yale is a client of the John Stevens Shop. Which, as it happens, is exactly where Zingo Stevens learned to cut letters in stone.

Tenk, tenk, tenk. Tenk, tenk. Tenk, tenk, tenk, tenk.

9

BALANCING ACT

Jamie Jauncey

I T'S THE YEAR 1715. In the Fife village of Auchtermuchty a blacksmith is shoeing a horse for his customer, a local farmer. The air is thick with rebellion. Fifteen miles away, in Perth, an army 8,000-strong is awaiting the arrival of the Highland clans, impatient to engage the forces of the Hanoverian government and restore the Stuarts, in the person of James Edward, the Old Pretender, to the British throne.

But just now the farmer couldn't care less about this doomed adventure. He has been to market to sell his barley, and he suspects he has been diddled. The blacksmith, who has prospered as much by being a good listener as a good artisan, continues to beat the glowing horseshoe into shape as his customer inveighs against the grain merchant's defective – or were they deliberately miscalibrated? – scales.

Weeks pass and one day the blacksmith calls the farmer into the depths of the smiddy. There he points to an elegant wrought-iron contraption hanging from the ceiling, its finely balanced cross-beam almost as wide as his outstretched arms. He has modelled it on the very latest German design, complete with knife-edge balance points for greater precision. Inlaid into the iron, in brass, is the date, 1715, and his name, John

White. There'll be no fiddling of the readings with this state-of-the-art device.

Perhaps this is how it happened, perhaps not ...

What is certain is that in that revolutionary year, John White, blacksmith of Auchtermuchty, made a set of scales that were the last word in weighing technology, and stamped them with his name and the date. Today, more than 300 years later, his great-great-great-great-great-grandson, Edwin White, shows them off to visitors at the premises of John White & Son, scalemakers of Auchtermuchty.

The smiddy has now become a light industrial unit, the wrought iron has given way to stainless steel and other materials, avoirdupois has yielded to metric and the technology has changed from the mechanics of weight and counterweight to the electronics of pressure-measurement. But the essential business of Scotland's oldest family firm hasn't changed in three centuries. Those scales are always there, poised in the back of everyone's minds, a reminder that in the twenty-first century John White & Son continue to trade in fairness – some might even call it justice.

This is the story of a pre-industrial-era business that has managed to survive into the digital age by sticking to what it knows best. But that's not all. There has also been good fortune, good judgement and a few narrow squeaks along the way. And there's a surprising contemporary twist to the tale.

Back in the eighteenth century, meanwhile, the smiddy remained a hot and clangourous place as John the founder, his son Thomas and his grandson John continued to craft their products at the forge. But change was in the air. By the time the great-grandson, Andrew, had come of age, the Industrial

Revolution was under way, anvils were falling silent as cast iron started to replace wrought iron and John White & Son was becoming an established business.

In the early nineteenth century, with smokestacks belching and the railways starting to connect even the most far-flung corners of the country with the great industrial centres, the market for precision casting was growing rapidly. Throughout this Victorian age, Andrew, his son John and his grandsons Andrew and Henry (the sixth generation) oversaw a century of steady expansion as they responded to the ever more varied needs of their customers the length of the United Kingdom. The machine age was upon them and those machines had a vast hunger for intricate and finely balanced working parts.

By now they were not only producing weighing machines of all sizes, in both brass and iron, but their workforce also included locksmiths, gunsmiths and general metalworkers, supplying goods as varied as fireplaces, iron railings, tea chests and even a small flat scale with a rod and scoop for measuring snuff.

The laws of the land were working in their favour, too, as industrial expansion and mass production heralded a new era in regulation. The Weights & Measures Acts (1878–93) introduced national standards for weighing machines, enforceable by local inspectors. For a firm with a reputation for reliable, high-quality weighing machines, this was a bonanza.

In order to fulfil demand while avoiding capital risk, the canny Whites persuaded an iron founder from Kirkcaldy to open a foundry next door to their factory. By the late nineteenth century, the small, sleepy, rural town of Auchtermuchty had become a bustling, noisy hive of industry, the twin peaks of the nearby Lomond Hills frequently obscured by the smoke that billowed from the tall brick chimneys of both the John White & Son scaleworks and the neighbouring Robert Ferlie & Sons foundry.

But the White family was out of balance. Shortly before the turn of the century, John and William, two sons of Andrew, the older of the two brothers then in charge, left the firm to set up in competition, a few hundred yards down the road. History doesn't relate what caused the rift, but after a number of years competing head to head with the senior firm in Auchtermuchty, White Brothers & Co., as the upstarts had named themselves, moved their business to Glasgow. There they continued to trade until the 1960s, when Andrew, the son of the defecting brother John, sold the business back to John White & Son, the circle completed.

War has always brought challenge and opportunity in equal measure for manufacturers of essential materiel. During the First World War, as shells without number rained down on the Western Front, the Ministry for Munitions issued an edict reserving brass for the manufacture of ordnance. The crafty Whites wrote to the Ministry for Munitions with a series of patterns for the most indispensable types of scales, and a request for the material necessary to produce them – which was duly granted. As their contribution to the war effort, the Whites produced a mammoth set of beam scales for weighing howitzer shells. A photograph shows them poised like some vast instrument of Judgement Day, dwarfing the flat-capped worker who stands alongside.

Business continued to boom during the inter-war period. In 1922 John White & Son opened their own foundry, at the back of the scaleworks. A decade later, spotting a gap for a specialised

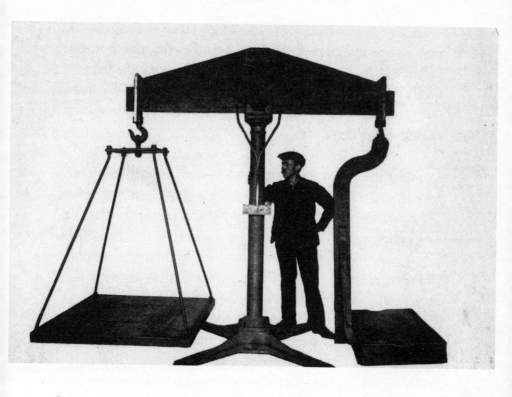

Large beam-scales for weighing Howitzer shells.

procedure beyond the competence of lesser casting works, they started a lucrative new line in moulds for glass bottles – including one for Coca-Cola. Another burgeoning source of income was the ongoing maintenance and calibration of the increasingly sophisticated weighing machines they were now selling to their customers.

Large families seem to have been a feature of the White line. Between 1739 and the mid-nineteenth century, four successive owners of the business between them produced thirty-one children, thus greatly increasing the likelihood that there would be at least one in each generation who would be interested, willing and competent to enter the family firm (an advantage denied to most smaller, modern families).

The seventh generation of Whites, brothers Andrew and Edwin, respectively the ninth and tenth of ten siblings, ran the business jointly into the mid-twentieth century. Their older brother, John, had briefly set up on his own in Edinburgh, but later rejoined the family firm and his enterprise became John White & Son's Edinburgh branch, with premises on Victoria Street, where they continued to sell scales and shop fittings of all kinds until 1978.

During the Second World War, their reputation for quality landed John White & Son a government contract to cast brake drums for Spitfires. By now they were making everything from kitchen scales to heavy industrial platforms. The post-war period also saw worldwide export sales booming as they adapted their products to foreign systems of measurement. A further lucrative product line emerged, this time from the whisky industry. Bottling plants needed a way to make the final check that there were no broken or missing contents once the six- or twelve-bottle cardboard packing cartons had been sealed. The Whites' response was the Cartomat (a name worthy of its era, the 1970s). This weighed each carton as it passed along the packing line and was later refined to divert underweight cartons onto a separate line for checking. In due course, almost all the major distillers came to install John White & Son's Cartomat. It was a timely development as UK manufacturers were beginning to face stiff competition from the cheap, volume-produced weighing products now flooding in from the Far East.

By now the eighth generation of Whites was running the company and the move from mechanical to electronic machines had begun, a step almost as monumental as that from the horse to the internal combustion engine. In 1994, Henry, the oldest of this generation, retired and sold the business to his two younger first cousins, John and Edwin. With a background in both mechanical engineering and electronics, John was well qualified to design the firm's new products and oversee the transition to the new technology.

Once again, however, a rift opened up and John and Edwin parted company. A game of musical chairs ensued. Under the name John White Automation Ltd, John continued to occupy the original premises, until eventually moving six miles down the road from Auchtermuchty to the equally small town of Markinch. After nearly 250 years of continuous occupation by the Whites, the original premises were sold to a property developer and later converted into a block of twelve flats and a house, with the dubious names of Whites Weigh and Y Weight.

Meanwhile, Edwin and his wife Tio kept the original business, now trading as John White & Son (Weighing Machines) Ltd, and moved into new premises in Auchtermuchty. Edwin had joined the family firm on graduating from university at the age of twenty-one, but nothing had prepared him for the challenge of taking it over in the midst of the transition to the new digital technology. The entire staff needed retraining and there was the inevitable pain, particularly acute in a small family business, of accepting that some people were not up to the challenge. For Tio, an artist by vocation, the world of business was unknown territory and the boundary between family friend and employee, both of which descriptions were true of most of the twenty or so staff, at first seemed a hard one to manage.

By 1997, crisis point was looming. Edwin and Tio went looking for help.

Auchtermuchty has long been burdened with a reputation for a certain kind of clichéd Scottishness. The home of both Jimmy Shand, whose kilted, accordion-playing statue graces a small community park, and those indefatigable walkers, The Proclaimers (no statue yet), it also suffers from a name which sounds to the unfamiliar ear like a mouthful of neeps. To the veteran *Daily Express* columnist Sir John Junor, Auchtermuchty was a kind of Brigadoon, 'a place of solemn courtesy to one's betters and implacable hostility to outsiders'.

Undeserved though this reputation may be, Auchtermuchty is still not a place where one would expect to walk into a small office and find a Kenyan woman and her two sons among the twenty-strong workforce. Yet it was Joyce Onuonga who answered Edwin and Tio's call for help in 1997.

At that time she had recently moved to Scotland to join her husband who was completing a doctorate at the University of St Andrews. Joyce herself had a background in business and education. She had also always possessed an irrepressibly entrepreneurial streak, first evidenced at boarding school in

Nairobi where, she relates with a grin, she used to make up her own beauty oils and charge her room-mates one Kenyan shilling apiece to braid their hair by candlelight. Later she went on to run her own business, exporting Kenyan products to Europe and North America.

Tio and Joyce met by chance. Soon Joyce was consulting for John White & Son, helping them to undertake the vital restructuring needed to ease their passage into the twenty-first century. Here was someone who brought to the business a set of different and much-needed skills, along with the objectivity that so easily eludes those who are entrenched in old practices and bear the weight of history on their shoulders. Before long, Edwin and Tio had decided on the unthinkable and made her a director of the company and the first ever non-family member to own shares in the business.

But Joyce Onuonga's involvement with John White & Son didn't end there.

Following that difficult patch in the late 1990s, Edwin, Tio and Joyce went on together to consolidate the firm's reputation for state-of-the-art digital weighing machines. Gone were the mechanical scales, banished by minutely sensitive electronic pressure pads. Today John White & Son supply everything from laboratory scales to automated, driver-controlled weighbridges whose readings are instantaneously uploaded to the customer company's database. For Forbo Flooring Systems, successor to the nineteenth-century Nairn linoleum empire and one of the Whites' oldest customers, they added the pleasingly eccentric touch of a retro red telephone box to house the weighbridge scanning gear and keep the truck drivers dry in bad weather. It's hard to imagine a multi-national corporation indulging in anything so whimsical.

Housing for Forbo Flooring Systems' weighbridge scanning equipment.

Now, at the time of writing, the order book is healthy, the future looks promising, the surprise ending to this chapter in the history of John White & Son has been sprung and a new one is unfolding. Edwin and Tio White are relinquishing control of the company and Joyce Onuonga is taking it over. The family is retaining a small stake in the business and Edwin and Tio will remain involved for a few more years in a non-executive capacity to support Joyce and her team. In 2017, its 302nd year, the venture started by a Fife blacksmith and managed for seven successive generations by his direct descendants is passing into the hands of a Kenyan business woman.

Edwin and Tio are happy, perhaps even relieved, at this extraordinary turn of events. At seventy-two, Edwin has had more than half a century of John White & Son and is understandably ready to hang up his hat. His children from his first marriage have made their own lives and have no involvement in the company. He and Tio have the satisfaction of knowing that they saved the business with their decision to break the tradition of seven generations and admit someone from outside the family on an equal footing to their own. They also know that Joyce's connection with the business and its eighteen members of staff goes back twenty years. They are her family, too, and she will look after them.

What is the secret of John White & Son's success to date? How has this small family firm, in its rural Scottish setting, survived for so long? 'Justice and equity make for a precise craft,' Edwin White reflects. In other words, there's no room for mistakes when it comes to measuring things, and the Whites have seldom put a foot wrong on that score. Independent-mindedness has played its part, too. Blacksmiths are a notoriously thrawn lot and perhaps that quality is embedded in the White

Edwin White, Tio White and Joyce Onuonga.

genes. Over the years they have turned down their fair share of offers for the business. They have also been lucky in that a member of each generation has proved to be a capable manager, and they have never fallen victim to the three-generation cycle of start-it, build-it, spend-it that comes to afflict so many family businesses. By the same token, they have also managed to survive their fair share of family shenanigans. As Edwin points out, things often get tricky when cousins are involved, but in their case the rifts have ended up working to their advantage, with the breakaway businesses eventually coming back into their hands again. One man's luck is another man's judgement, and a reputation for shrewdness is nothing new to the inhabitants of the Kingdom of Fife.

And what of John White & Son's new family from across the water, the new dynasty as embodied by Joyce and her sons? Joyce's energy and enthusiasm are palpable. For its size, the firm makes an already substantial commitment to research and development, and her sights are set on the new niches they can create through innovation. In an age of measurement, accountability, transparency and evaluation, the climate already favours those in the business of precision. The next challenge, she believes, is to capture efficiently the blizzard of valuable data that ensues from all that measuring. John White & Son's existing and potential customers can expect to hear a good deal more about that in the months and years to come.

When she declares that they are setting up Scotland's oldest family business for the next 300 years, one is inclined to believe her. She speaks regularly to her father in Kenya. 'You are carrying Scottish history,' he tells her. 'It is a great honour.' Joyce Onuonga does not demur.

10

CREAM RISES TO THE TOP

Mike Gogan

It's 11:45 p.m. on 31 December 2016.

ROBBIE MINTO MOVES HIS CHERRY PICKER into position at the granite arch of St James's Gate, Dublin. He is the man responsible for a most public display of Guinness's longevity. Carrying on a long-standing tradition, each New Year's Eve he changes one of the two dates that adorn the respective sides of the arch. The other date, 1759, remains.

His little piece of theatre has an audience. A crowd grows in excitement on the street below. They grow in number, too, spreading across Thomas Street to where a plaque commemorates another event, when a 'Mr Kernan turned and walked down the slope of Watling Street by the corner of Guinness's visitors' waiting room' (James Joyce, *Ulysses*).

Ten members of Robbie's extended family count down
to midnight below him on the pavement.
Nine times he checks his watch for good measure.
Eight cameras at the ready.
Seven years now Robbie has presided over this date
ceremony and it always gives him a thrill.

Six screws to hand to secure the new date plaque in place.
Five turns of each to make sure.
Four seconds to go.
Three cheers for Robbie and his mate.
Two yellow hats raised in salute to the two date panels.
One reads 1759, the other 2017.
Happy New Year from Guinness.

From his vantage point, Robbie views Guinness's success as having little to do with leaps in innovation and technology over the last quarter of a millennium. Yes, it's a long way from Arthur Guinness's first wooden-vatted brewhouse to Diageo's fourth-generation, stainless steel, automated brewing plant. Yet at the core of this business is an iconic pint of beer that has not changed much in more than 200 years. That pint, according to Robbie, is consistency – bottled, canned or draught.

Ironically, a drink is the one thing missing from the little celebration outside the brewery gates at midnight. Nobody among the loyal band of Dubliners who turn up here is raising a glass. Some are young, some are old, some drunk, some sober. All are curious. Like the retired newspaper photographer who proudly tells me he has a photographic record of the changing of the date at St James's Gate for each of the last twenty-five years.

All will raise a glass later. It's New Year's Eve after all. It's Ireland after all. It's Guinness after all these years.

These Dubliners have witnessed the dawning of another year in the history of their relationship with Guinness. It's a symbiotic relationship. As another of Dublin's famous writers, Brendan Behan, said in response to a comment that Guinness has been good to the people of Dublin: 'and haven't the people of Dublin been good to Guinness?'

Itisthebrewerofthe Irish nation's oldestandmostfavoured drink other than a cup oftea; the city's largest employer oflucky generations of craftsmen; benefactor to employee, city, nation, economy; supporter of culture, art and sport; and entertainer of TV audiences with the ingenuity and wit of its advertising. Its name is that of the man forever famous as the founder of the business in 1759, the creator of the pint, the father of six generations of the one family to run this business.

Arthur Guinness was born in 1725 in the village of Celbridge in what is today, by happy coincidence, a pub. Celbridge is about twenty-five kilometres from the site of the modern brewery. Both locations are connected by the River Liffey which meanders slowly along its 'riverrun' towards Dublin Bay.

As a young man, Arthur Guinness bought a small brewery in nearby Leixlip, another village nestling further downstream on the Liffey. He funded it with a £100 inheritance from his godfather, an archbishop. Is the Church ever far away from a historical event in Ireland?

Arthur soon had his sights set farther downstream. Following the river to its mouth in Dublin, he took out his famous 9,000-year lease at £45 a year on a run-down brewery at St James's Gate in 1759.

This gate apparently takes its name from the holy well of St James which was located in the area, and was the starting point for one of the medieval pilgrimage routes to Santiago de Compostela, 'Santiago' being the Spanish form of 'Saint James'. Religion and history collaborate again in a story of Ireland and beer.

The course of Arthur's life may have been charted by the river and water that flow past the brewery's gates. But, contrary to popular belief, the Liffey is not the source of the water so essential to brewing Guinness. The eight million litres of water necessary per day flow instead from the Wicklow mountains above Dublin.

It was water that was the first of many challenges faced by Guinness along the course of its history. Among other things, Arthur's lease gave him free access and rights to a constant supply of running water. Sensing in 1773 that it had perhaps been overgenerous with its lease, Dublin Corporation decided to fill in the water course in question. Displaying what those who know today's Guinness brand values as inner strength and courage, Arthur himself seized one of the corporation men's pickaxes and threatened the team of workers. He must have made a stout impression because the group left without completing their work. It took twelve years for the dispute over water to settle, yet settle it did like a good pint of draught, in 1785.

That essential water, yeast, malted barley and hops are the living elements of Guinness – the same ingredients today as they were two and a half centuries ago. They have endured and survived in a secret recipe that earns the resulting pint a place in the hearts of beer aficionados the world over.

They say (whoever *they* are) that the yeast used in Guinness comes from the strain that Arthur Guinness himself used. Who can tell fact from legend? What we do know is that since before the 1900s generation after generation of brewers use a little yeast from each brew in the next to ensure consistency. That same strain of yeast is grown only in St James's Gate, with a reserve supply kept in the director's safe.

Arthur's legacy is one of the oldest breweries in the world, a business run with what seems to be enduring ingredients for success.

No less tangible than what goes into making Guinness, philanthropy, benevolence, a strong sense of family, business acumen, an appetite for change and challenge, and courage are some of the qualities that have made Guinness stand head and shoulders (well, head, anyway) above other beers for so long.

Family first. The Guinnesses were a Protestant family with Quaker leanings, claiming Catholic descent in a country divided by centuries-long Anglo-Irish strife. These contradictions seemed to fuel an energy that runs throughout Guinness history, usually to its benefit.

Arthur himself was the first philanthropist of the family. He gave generously to charity, but it was his great-grandson, Edward Cecil Guinness (later Lord Iveagh), who left his mark so significantly on Dublin. He lent his name to the Iveagh Trust buildings, fine red-bricked 'flats' that line Dublin streets, originally built as affordable, clean housing for Dublin's working class; to Iveagh Markets, built to keep street traders out of the weather; and to Iveagh Gardens, a hidden gem of a public park, designated as a National Historic Property. He contributed to institutions for scientific research, libraries and public baths. His older brother, Arthur Edward Guinness, Lord Ardilaun, paid for the development of St Stephen's Green, bequeathing it to the city once it was completed. Today as a beautifully planted public park in the middle of the chic shopping area, it is where the Dubs (as we refer to ourselves) feed ducks and catch the rare rays of warm sunshine enjoyed by the city.

There is real business acumen in this family, too, first displayed in Arthur's famous foresight with the St James's Gate lease. Throughout its history, the board, on which sat a direct descendant of Arthur's until Benjamin Guinness retired in 1986, was scrupulous in its financial dealings. From 1759

St James's Gate, Thomas Street, Dublin. As it was, is and ever shall be...

until Guinness was floated in 1886, profits were continually reinvested in expanding the business, or in schemes to benefit the employees and the city of Dublin. Even the building of Park Royal brewery in London in the early 1930s was financed from the firm's own resources.

But no matter how sophisticated a business Guinness became, it remained true to Arthur's core objective of brewing, selling and exporting porter. We know from his original brewing notebooks that he experimented with different measurements of hops and malted barley to create variants and refinements. Today these priceless notebooks, with their neat rows of figures first set down in 1796, are proving the inspiration for new recipes developed by brewers at Guinness.

Perhaps it was his experiments, so carefully recorded, that led Arthur to abandon the brewing of ale in 1799 in favour of porter. Originally a brew for the porters of Covent Garden in London, Arthur perfected it and soon created West India Porter especially for export. It is still brewed today and is known as Guinness Foreign Extra Stout, responsible for 45 per cent of global sales, mainly in Asia, Africa and the Caribbean.

Arthur died in 1803, leaving a business that then passed from father to son for five successive generations. His son, Arthur II (one of twenty-one children), continued to develop the local and export business with new brews. One in particular became what we know today as Guinness Extra Stout or, to those who enjoy one of the three million of them brewed in Dublin each day, 'a pint of the black stuff'.

Arthur Guinness II presided over the company's growth to become the largest brewery in Ireland and a substantial export business. Within a hundred years of its foundation the brewery had doubled in size and had become increasingly important to the economy, with one in thirty people in Dublin depending on Guinness for a livelihood.

In the Guinness generations that followed, markets began to open and thrive around the globe. At the turn of the last century, 150 years into its history Guinness was well established as the biggest brewery in the world. The Dublin base was a city within a city and the capital's largest employer, with its own fleet of barges and steamships, a fire brigade, a dispensary and its own internal railway system – all streets ahead of what the host city could boast at the time.

In 1916, as war raged across Europe, Dublin was caught up in its own turmoil. The 1916 Easter Rising, the armed insurrection in which the Republic of Ireland was first proclaimed, was being fought in Dublin's streets. The brewery saw a little action. It took nothing worse than sniper fire from the nearby Roe's Distillery, which was occupied by Irish Volunteer rebels, among them my grandfather. With the permission of the board, British forces occupied the Maltstore at Robert Street within the brewery complex where two brewery men were killed by a British sergeant.

But while the brewery survived, other parts of Dublin suffered terrible destruction. The first European city centre ever to endure urban warfare, street-by-street, building-by-building, even hand-to-hand. It was the first also to be shelled by gunboat from the river and to suffer the firestorms that followed.

Today, one hundred years later, the scene is set for a vivid reminder of Guinness's good fortune. Directly across the river Liffey from the brewery, a stone-arched gateway leads into a former British Army barracks. I took my young son Liam through it to visit what is now the National Museum of Ireland,

The iron-clad oak vats of Arthur Guinness's first vat house. Still standing after all these years and functioning as an employee bike shed.

home to a new exhibit of the Easter Rising. There we viewed the names of his two great-grandfathers on the official roll of honour of those who took part.

On our way out, a stunning view of the Guinness brewery is framed by that stone arch. The modern Brewhouse 4, its sleek-edged bulk rises out of a vast 55-acre brewery site. An enormous Guinness harp symbol, first used in 1862 and trade-marked in 1876, sits proud of the massive black façade of the building. The back-lit, golden harp is set in mirror image to the national symbol of the Republic of Ireland, so closely are the two histories in tune.

The entire history of Guinness's survival is represented in the fabric of the buildings at the St James's Gate site: the sturdy brick walls of Vat House 1, where the original vats used by Arthur Guinness to mature beer are still standing, 200 years later; dry oak beams, rusting ironmongery, vast copper kettles, tiled subterranean passageways, stainless steel storage tanks, the laboratories, offices, marketing suites – all telling their parts of the story of the fluctuating fortunes of Guinness.

More challenge and trouble arrived in 1917 when Lloyd George introduced a wartime measure reducing the alcohol content of beer to no more than 5 per cent. The result for Guinness was a stout that was weaker, shorter in shelf life and less able to stand up to the rigorous movement of export by sea. The taste of Guinness suffered in Britain in the following years as the beer frequently failed to stay fresh on the journey from Dublin to England. The drinking public turned to other beers and sales fell. Before the brewers could find a way of prolonging shelf life, another blow came with the introduction of Prohibition in the USA, which had become a significant market. Then came the Great Depression, decimating the export bottling firms that Guinness relied on as distributors.

Now the solution fell not to the brewers, but to the brand. In the late 1920s, Lord Iveagh (the original Arthur's great-grandson) was still on the board at almost eighty years old. He had long believed that the beer should sell on its own merits, refusing permission to advertise on the grounds that to do so signified a problem. But he was eventually persuaded that you can talk your way out of trouble, thus opening the door to a campaign that was to make Guinness a household name.

The first of the famous Guinness advertisements arrived in 1929 with the slogan 'Guinness Is Good For You'. It stuck so well that expectant mothers and babies were often recommended a drop of Guinness for its apparent medicinal properties. John Gilroy, artist and writer at the S. H. Benson agency, followed the first advertisements in 1935 with his campaign of zoo animal characters, such as emus, toucans and seals, in 'My Goodness, My Guinness', a campaign that endured for more than thirty-five years.

But advertising alone could not sustain growth for ever, and sales began to fall again in the late 1950s as draught beers became popular and the pint glass threatened the traditional bottled beer market that Guinness had so successfully captured.

This time the solution lay with science. The brewery had undergone intense modernisation since the end of the Second World War, and the laboratory now found the means to win this latest market battle. Unlike other beers, Guinness didn't present at all well when it was first drawn from a keg. After a couple of years of research, featuring a variety of aluminium keg prototypes, the Easy Serve system emerged. Beer, carbon dioxide and nitrogen mixed as they exited a keg to produce Draught Guinness, one of the brand's great successes.

Two of Gilroy's iconic advertising images.

With it came an entire new vocabulary, creating a mysterious and alluring tone of anticipation and pleasure in the drinking of a pint. There is *The Call* (even faced with a bar counter forested with competing beer taps, simply saying 'a pint' is often a default call to get you a Guinness), *The Pour* (in two stages, of course), *The Wait* (causing anxiety among those unfamiliar with it and pleasure among those who are), *The Surge* (of tiny nitrogen bubbles as they appear to float down the glass), *The Settle* (two types here: one into black and white, the other the drinker settling into the pint itself), *The Rings* (of left-over head that mark the swallows down the emptying glass), *The Dregs* (not worth talking about) and finally *The Call* again (for another one, because a bird never flew on one wing).

Consumers' impatience rose to challenge Guinness again in the 1980s. The supermarket trade and the growing popularity of wine made drinking at home a new social norm. Pubs began to lose market share as people entertained at home. Guinness, dominant in a beer market, suffered heavily.

Within the technology that created Draught Guinness, there lay the means to restore the brand's fortunes once again. The ambition was to create the Draught Guinness experience in the comfort of the home. More intense technological investment and innovation led to the invention of the widget, essentially a tiny beer keg within a can. A small plastic bubble sealed inside the can contains nitrogen and beer. A change in pressure when the can is opened causes a valve in the widget to burst, releasing a spurt of nitrogen-charged beer into the can, multiplying the effect on the rest of the beer. Marketed in 1988, the widget in the can revitalised what had been a declining Draught Guinness.

If the longevity of Guinness can be put down to inner strength and courage, more of it rose to the top with Brewhouse 4. Opened in 2014, the computerised modernity of the new Brewhouse 4 has revitalised the fortunes of St James's Gate, which was rumoured to be set for closure soon after the creation in 1997 of Guinness's parent company Diageo, headquartered in London.

Today three million pints a day are brewed at St James's Gate. It is now the most technologically advanced brewery in the world, ensuring that nothing in the experience of the Guinness drinker changes. And that consistency is celebrated openly in the Guinness Storehouse, an extravagant visitor attraction. The circular viewing bar towering over the cityscape has helped it to become Ireland's most popular tourist experience.

So much has changed for Guinness over 258 years, yet there is so much to the beer that has not changed at all. Massive advances in technology have brought consistency so that we enjoy more or less the same iconic pint whether we are supping the strong, bittersweet taste of burnt caramel in a Foreign Extra Stout in Nigeria, or poising our upper lip over the cheese-like head of Draught Guinness in the Brazen Head, Dublin.

As Robbie Minto said, changing the date once again on New Year's Eve 2016, the reason behind Guinness's success is the pint itself. Since 1759, one beer has moved from barrel to bottle, from keg to glass, from bar to living room.

Today it is enjoyed in 150 countries, produced directly by five different breweries and under licence by another fifty. Wherever you drink Guinness you're enjoying one of the ten million pints drunk every day, each one as good as the last, each one true to its founder's vision.

Good to the last drop.
Enjoy.

11

PIONEER SPIRIT

Mark Watkins

Timeline

1824: The Australian Agricultural Company (AACo) is established by Act of British Parliament, granting it a million acres of land in the colony of New South Wales for sheep farming.

1825: Robert Dawson, AACo's 'Chief Agent', sets sail from England with a retinue of staff and initial breeding stock.

1829: With the venture struggling, Dawson is dismissed and replaced by Sir Edward Parry, who is credited with saving the company.

1831: Drought and the unsuitability of the million acres for sheep farming sees the initial land grant exchanged for other plots.

1850: Sheep numbers rise to 114,118, cattle to 8,306 and horses to 1,436. Cattle sales are largely domestic, but wool and horse sales provide export income.

WWI: A labour shortage and wool taxes force AACo to move away from sheep towards cattle production.

1916: The company moves north, selling its southern land to finance territory in Queensland and, later, Northern Territory.

WWII: Labour shortages and lack of income from wool accelerate the shift from sheep to cattle.

Early 1950s: UK exports dwindle but US sales grow.

Early 1970s: A beef price crash threatens the company, but it sees out the crisis.

1985: More land sales and purchases. Final phasing out of sheep farming.

1996: The last part of the original million acres is sold, after 165 years.

2000: The cattle herd size reaches 363,000 with sales to Australia, Asia, America and the Middle East.

2016: AACo owns or leases close to 18 million acres across more than twenty properties - more than 1 per cent of the entire Australian landmass.

R ESEARCH SOMETIMES takes us to strange places and uncovers unexpected voices. My search for the story of the Australian Agricultural Company led me to dusty archives, connected me with encyclopaedic academics and took me on a pilgrimage to where the company really started, in rural New South Wales. To bring this history to life, I have channelled the voices of those who were there at the time, in a series of recreated notes and correspondence. But for these people, both notable and ordinary, the AACo might well have died at birth. That it still exists nearly two hundred years later is a testament to them and those who followed in their footsteps.

Leadership

London, December 1824

Beloved Wife,

Such news. I have this day accepted the situation of Chief Agent for the Australian Agricultural Company, a new business venture to be established by an eminent group of gentlemen led by none other than my old school friend Mr John Macarthur junior.

These past years have been so hard on us and if the price of agricultural produce does not improve, I fear for the future of farming in England.

So, I sense the hand of fate in this exciting new turn of events, and the flatlands of the Essex countryside will become a distant memory within the year, for my new situation requires me to establish and administer agriculture on one million acres in the colony of New South Wales.

There is already much to do. Mr Macarthur must secure the assent of parliament for the new company. Given that he counts parliamentarians, aristocrats and officers of the East India Company among his investors, he is openly confident of success.

Meanwhile, I must busy myself with engaging the services of shepherds, stable hands, carpenters and all manner of tradesmen who are both willing to join us on this venture and who have the fortitude to guarantee its success. Then there is the small matter of acquiring the livestock to establish ourselves in the colony, not to mention securing the passage south for man and creature. I venture to guess that we will need to secure two ships at least if we are to arrive with satisfactory resources for the venture.

I will return home in a day or two, once I have made some initial preparations. Until then, I send my love to you my darling.

Affectionately yours, your husband
Robert Dawson

Robert Dawson was a landowner who was sought out by AACo to lead their new venture. In correspondence, they describe him as: 'a gentleman whose respectability, talents, and extensive agricultural as well as general experience, eminently qualify him for the duties he has undertaken'.

Recruitment

Ship 'York', October 1825

Dearest Mother,

I take my pen in hand to write with the most grievous news.
James has been taken from us. It happened during a fearful
storm one night aboard the York, perhaps three weeks into
our voyage. It was as if the very hand of God were stirring
the waves into a frenzy. There was such terrible bleating and
pleading from the animals, as if they spoke what we could
not bring ourselves to say out loud: 'please save us, make this
end, toss us not to our deaths.'

James, bless his soul, took to the deck to see if there was
anything to be done. To a man, the crew was as white as the
sails in full sunlight. James has never been one for the water,
except for a hip bath once a week, and his fear was plain
to see, but he was a man who always wanted to be doing
something rather than nothing, which I suppose is why he
went out onto deck.

I did not see it, but a midshipman says he saw James swallowed
by a wave big as a whale and, when it washed away, he was
gone. The crew called out and threw ropes overboard, but all
they pulled back was salt-soaked hemp.

Despair, to which I have hitherto been a stranger, has taken possession of me and an awful emptiness has overtaken little Emma. When she sleeps, which is rarely, I sit lonely as a gull on the mast, wondering when landfall will come and what it will mean for me now, widowed with child. We are now but a few weeks from Sydney, without James and with no salary to keep us in the new lands. Without money, a return passage is out of the question and we will be cast away in New South Wales as surely as if the ship had broken its back in that terrible storm.

By the time we make port, my husband will be half the world away, at the bottom of the ocean with all our hopes for this life. Now we know not what the future holds, so pray for us dear mother. Pray.

Respectfully, your daughter
Elizabeth Carter

James Carter was to be a miller for the AACo. Elizabeth remarried in New South Wales within a year.

The northern shore of Port Stephens, where beach
gives way to marsh and scrub.

Launch

Extracts from the journal of William Telfer.

---

*The land grant the Company has taken lies to the north of
Port Stephens, a pleasant harbour a day's sailing north of
Sydney. The harbour itself is bounded by sandy beaches and
low marshland giving way to dense primeval forest and lofty
hills. The Company has taken possession of a million acres
of what lies before us, for the purposes of sheep grazing and
wool production.*

———

*Where we first came ashore, a settlement named Carrabean
has been established comprising habitation, stores, warehouses, hospital and a chapel. Further settlements demon-
strate the Company's hope that our farming here will be
as successful as that in England's rich west, and north of
Carrabean we will establish Stroud and Gloucester as the
Company's main centres. A road will also be cut so that travel
between each place may take less than a day.*

———

*The land here proves difficult for sheep farming. Since our
arrival, New South Wales has had to contend with one of the
most fearful droughts the Earth has seen since the days of the
Pharaohs. Privately, many of the men believe the Company's
choice of land to have been a poor one. The ground is either
marshy, or bad and stony. Inland, the terrain is mountainous in
places and extremely scrubby, covered with stunted trees and
wild undergrowth such that it is unfit for almost anything. While
Carrabean, Stroud and Gloucester will stand as monuments*

to all that is English, what surrounds them is foreign to us and confounds all that we know of sheep-herding.

———

The Company will not permit an inn on its Estate for fear of drunkenness & disorderly conduct. Indeed, the keeper of a public house in Stroud was asked to wind up his business and move away after the sale of spirituous liquors saw the Stroud School damaged and the Company's business, such as it is, neglected.

William Telfer was a shepherd for the AACo who also sailed on the York with Robert Dawson and James and Elizabeth Carter. He was still with the company under Edward Parry in 1833, by which time he had risen to be overseer of sheep. Carrabean was later renamed Carrington and still exists today.

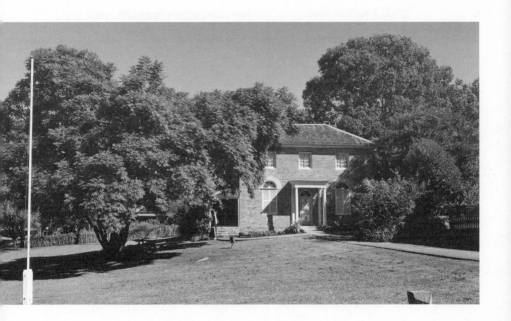

The school house at Stroud still stands, despite
the drunken revelries of the 1820s.

Progress Report

Parramatta, March 1828

GENTLEMEN,

I have deferred my Report to you on the state of the
Company's Establishment at Port Stephens until the present
time in the hope of obtaining further and more satisfactory
explanations than have yet been received from Mr. Dawson.
Now, I can no longer postpone submitting to your notice a
brief statement of my observations.

On 29th December I visited Stroud. Mr. George Jenkins,
general superintendent of all the sheep accompanied me. The
first flock we saw was in good condition, the second looked
tolerably well, but the third appeared to me to be nearly in
a hopeless state. Further flocks were either in reduced or
miserably low condition.

The Overseer in charge of these flocks is a native of Berkshire
named Titcombe. I do not doubt he may possess a competent
knowledge of the duties of an English South Down Shepherd;
but it is obvious he can as yet have but little experience of the
treatment of sheep in New South Wales.

I am at a loss to account for the deterioration and extensive
mortality that have taken place since my last visit. Mr. Dawson
attributes it to the livestock's old age, and to the sufferings

undergone during the voyage, but I cannot help thinking that
there must also have been mismanagement or neglect. Indeed, it
is evident that little of Mr. Dawson's attention has been bestowed
upon the sheep.

The only course that can be adopted, to protect the interests
of the Company, is to nominate a deputation to proceed to
Port Stephens for the purpose of a full inquiry into the state of
the Establishment and the conduct of Mr. Dawson.

I have the honour to be,
Gentlemen,
With great regard,
Your obedient Servant,
JAMES MCARTHUR

James McArthur was a constant thorn in Dawson's side and
seems to have conspired to bring him down, being involved
in the sale of substandard stock to AACo at inflated prices and
then blaming Dawson in a lengthy report to his brother and the
AACo directors in London.

Corporate Culture

Extracts from the journal of William Telfer.

This land appears greedy for the corpses of the young. This past morning it has taken the soul of a shepherd's son, little more than a year old, along with five of the lambs born this past week. It pains me to say such a thing but the shepherd could bear the loss of his child but he fell to his knees at the sight of the five lambs. Perchance it may have been the general effect of all the losses, or perchance those lambs said more to him about our prospects here than the death of his own little one, but despair walks among us like a black crow, cawing and eyeing which dwellings to alight upon next.

———

Being situated at the opposite extremity of the globe, our seasons are nearly the reverse of those in England. Our December, January, and February, are summer, when the atmosphere is heated and exhausting, while winter falls in June, July and August. Christmas at the height of summer is a strange affair indeed and by time evening comes, celebration and revelry is far from our minds. Dust coats our warm faces, we are gasping for breath and mosquitoes and sand-flies worry us at all points, so that at length all we can do is throw ourselves on the mattress beneath the mosquito-curtains.

———

One of the McArthur family came a-calling, full of 'why this' and 'on whose authority.' He travelled up the valley from Carrabean to Stroud, stopping at every flock on the way, inspecting every building and questioning near every man to work for the Company. He seems taken with the idea that moneys were spent that should not have been, and tasks were not undertaken that should have been. Mr. Dawson did not accompany him and the situation had the air of a spy come among us with the purpose of uncovering secrets.

———

Word has come that Mr. Dawson has been summoned to London to give account of our situation. There is talk that the Company may abandon its venture here, and we know little of what that might mean for those of us who have thrown ourselves in with Mr. Dawson. True, there can be little said for Mr. Dawson's choice of land, and the prospects for our flocks remain uncertain, but drought, pests and hardship in such large measure were not to be reckoned with and we have surely learnt much these past years that would offer us hope for the future. To give up now and quit this place would mean it has all been for nought.

Succession Planning

Port Stephens, January 1829

Beloved Wife,

Forgive the quality of the ink and paper, but I write this urgently so that it might find passage back to you in the hands of a traveller about to board the Lambton, bound for Sydney.

Much has changed since my last letter. John Macarthur's brother, James, visited our holdings a month past. I have written to you before of my concerns about his interests and interventions in the affairs of the Company under his authority as a member of the local Committee of Management.

Following his visit, James McArthur drafted a letter with a great many damaging reports about our situation here, the state of the flocks and about my personal conduct as Agent for the Company.

The Directors have responded by recalling me to London to give an account of my conduct and the Company's affairs, but I fear their minds are already made up and my position here will meet its end upon my return.

I implore you to delay your plans to join me in New South Wales with our children. We shall be together again soon, not, as anticipated, under southern skies, but amid the kinder climate of England, and I cannot say I am sorry for it, for the trials of these past few years have been remorselessly hard to bear.

Affectionately yours, your husband
Robert Dawson

Managing Change

Ship William, Port Jackson

23rd December 1829

To the Committee of Management of the Australian
Agricultural Company, Sydney

Gentlemen,

I beg to acquaint you with my arrival here this day in the Ship
William and have the honour to enclose herewith a Letter
from the Directors of the Australian Agricultural Company in
London, informing you of my appointment as Commissioner
with full powers for managing their affairs in New South Wales.

I beg to assure you that I shall feel greatly obliged by any
advice and information with which you may do me the favour
to furnish me, and which, from your superior knowledge
and experience in such matters, cannot fail to be of essential
assistance to me in the important duties I have undertaken
to perform.

Sir Edward Parry,
Commissioner to the Australian Agricultural Company

From the Personal Notebook of Sir Edward Parry

Items of principal importance
  I. *Restore and maintain due order in the Company's establishments*
 II. *Review the situation of the Company's million acre Grant on the northern shores of Port Stephens and arrange an exchange of lands if necessary*
III. *Negotiate with the Colonial Government over the management of coal mines.*

The Arctic explorer Sir Edward Parry arrived in Carrabean to take over from Dawson in 1830. The local committee, of which James McArthur had been a member, was abolished and Parry assumed full responsibility for AACo's operations in New South Wales.

Outlook Statement

Tracing the origins of the Australian Agricultural Company has been a little like turning detective. Although the company was born in London, Stroud is where it found its feet, and, at every turn, there are markers and mementoes of its time here.

In many ways Stroud could be a museum town. The original AACo buildings – school, workers' cottages, administrative buildings, courthouse, general store, grain silos – are all still here. The company is long gone, of course. In time, it probably came to see Port Stephens and its related settlements as a folly that nearly strangled the company at birth.

But it's here that the company was established, where it foundered, survived and eventually found its way out of.

It turned out that Robert Dawson lacked the knowledge and ability to choose land suitable for sheep farming. His dismissal and replacement with Sir Edward Parry – an Arctic explorer, former Royal Navy officer and staunch disciplinarian – saw a turnaround in AACo's fortunes.

It was surviving those fragile first decades here that enabled AACo to take advantage of the good luck that followed – exchanging its properties around Stroud for better land to the north and west; taking over the Newcastle coal mines so its income streams weren't wholly reliant on the price of wool; and eventually abandoning sheep farming altogether in favour of cattle. But all that has its roots here and came from the appointment of Parry.

There's something else, too, and I found it in the churchyard. There lie the graves of the men, women and children who placed their belief in AACo, Dawson, Parry and others. They weren't here to make a return on their investment capital, or to grab vast tracts of colonial land. They were here to survive – scratching a living out of the bare rocks and soil, bracing themselves against unpredictable elements and shutting their ears to strange noises as they tried to convince themselves that this was the West of England, not the edge of the known world.

They were human resources in its most literal form and they frequently paid the highest price imaginable.

The landscape of Stroud and the other AACo towns – Tahlee, Carrington, Booral, Stratford, Gloucester, Tamworth – may have been funded from London, but it was paid for here, in sweat and bones by people whose names are barely recalled.

As with all history, little evidence of their stories remains and I have had to imagine their accounts to lend colour to the otherwise dry records and correspondence of AACo and its senior managers.

What made this company a success? You can point to many things over a near 200-year history, but I think that its history would have been much shorter but for three things – the investors kept their nerve when they could easily have lost it; then, whatever the politics involved (and there were plenty), sacking Dawson in favour of Parry seems to have pulled things back from the brink; but most of all, and perhaps the one we can learn from in this age of 'employee engagement', 'discretionary effort' and all of that other twenty-first-century management-speak, is the fact that AACo was built on the efforts of workers who gave everything to make it a success.

I came here looking for traces of the birth of a company. I am leaving with images of those people's graves in my head. AACo's ancestors lie here, but I think they'd be proud to know that the company they helped to establish is still around, and that its long history brought me here to uncover their stories.

They came in wooden ships with their cows and sheep to start anew. What they started survives to this day. That's a legacy surely anyone would be proud of.

Thank you for helping their story to live on.

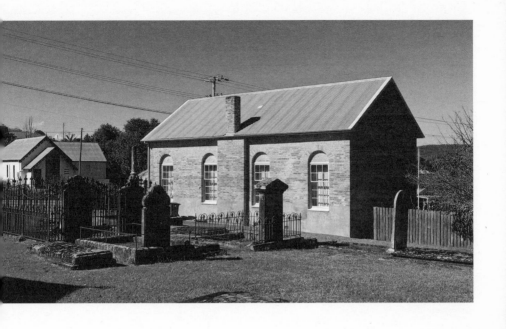

Stroud's cemetery bears witness to the town's early
settlers and their sacrifices.

12

STICK TO YOUR PRINCIPLES

Andy Milligan

IN 1891, WILLIAM WRIGLEY JR left his birthplace of Pennsylvania for the city of Chicago. He was an ambitious twenty-nine-year-old determined to make his name in the world. He arrived in the Windy City with $32 in his pocket and a dream in his head. That $32 would be worth roughly $800 in today's money. He was not therefore an enormously wealthy man whose parents could loan him, say, the equivalent of $1m to start a real estate business. But what he lacked in resources he made up for in gumption, in staying power and in a set of values to which he would stick for the rest of his life. They are values with which he imbued the eponymous business he created: Wrigley.

When he died in 1932, aged seventy, his $32 had grown into an estimated personal fortune of $34m. His name had also become one of the most famous in the world. Wrigley products are now sold in 180 countries and made in 140 factories across the globe. In Chicago, the Wrigley Building is an iconic landmark on the city's Magnificent Mile and Wrigley Field is the home of the Chicago Cubs baseball team.

But William Wrigley's path to glory was a combination of accident and foresight that accelerated the growth of a product that the world chews.

His father had a business selling scouring soaps and so, with his modest $32 investment, William first began selling the family products. He must have assumed that, with its rivers running fetid with the discarded carcasses from the burgeoning meat factories, a rapidly industrialising city like Chicago would be in need of a good wash. But business was competitive and slow. So, with an eye for marketing promotion that would be a continuous feature of his later company, he began to introduce incentives, bonuses or 'giveaways' with Wrigley's Scouring Soap.

One of his first 'giveaways' was a sachet of baking powder. He soon discovered, however, that the baking powder was more popular than the soap. So he switched production and his brand to the baking powder. To encourage sales of the baking powder, he started to give away two sticks of chewing gum. Then he discovered that the gum was even more popular than the baking powder. So he switched production again, and the now legendary Wrigley chewing gum was born.

A Short History of Chewing Gum

Human beings have been chewing gum for millennia. According to Wrigley's own website, the ancient Greeks chewed gum formed from the bark of the mastic tree found mainly in Greece and Turkey, hence our English word 'mastication'. Greek women chewed mastic gum to clean their teeth. Native Americans used to chew the resin from spruce trees when they were thirsty. In fact, spruce gum was the first chewing gum to be sold as a commercial product early in the 1800s.

Over the years, other substances have been used as chewing gum, many of them from the barks of trees. Chicle, which comes from the milky juice (latex) of the sapodilla tree found in South America, was especially popular. However, as demand for gum increased, it proved impossible to supply it in sufficient quantity using natural resources.

Consequently, the most enduring and widely used gums have been synthetic. For example, paraffin-based gums were popular at one stage. The first patent for chewing gum was granted to William Semple, an Ohio dentist, in 1869. It was to make gum from rubber which then became the dominant synthetic format. But Semple never sold a single stick of gum. In fact, John Curtis established the first successful production process, a process that is still used today. The gum base is melted down at temperatures of up to 240 degrees, thus sterilising it. It is then poured into vast mixers where the various flavours and sweeteners are added. Next the combined ingredients are allowed to cool till they form something like a huge 'loaf' of gum. That loaf is then sent through a series of rollers, each of which gradually thins the gum into a long ribbon shape. This is then cut into appropriate sizes for consumption. Syrup mixtures, each containing a different flavouring ingredient, are then used to cover the gum. Finally, it's packaged, put on pallets and sent out of the factory door.

John Curtis, however, was not exceptionally successful. The first commercially successful mass production was developed by Thomas Adams, whose American Chicle company still trades today. Wrigley's manufacturing process is in essence the same although much more efficient and productive because of its investment in technology. Nevertheless, today it still takes thirty-four hours to produce a stick of gum in Wrigley's state-of-the-art factories.

What Makes Wrigley Special?

William Wrigley was therefore the first neither to invent gum nor to mass-produce it. But he created the most successful gum company in the world. Why? Because he was an innovative and insightful marketer who had a few simple beliefs to which he stuck throughout his life. These beliefs have survived him and live on in the company. They still drive the brand's activities.

One of Wrigley's early insights that led to an enduring belief is the importance of 'strong taste' for a gum. Taste in a gum is very important because it can only last for a short while – much less than the time taken to chew the gum. Typically, the taste of gum disappears after five minutes, leaving just the satisfaction – and the saliva – of the act of chewing itself. Wrigley therefore understood the need to make the taste strong and long-lasting. A 'taste sensation', in fact, has been the hallmark of all of the brand's most popular products. The first two product brands Wrigley launched were called Lotta and Vassar but it was his next two, Juicy Fruit (now the longest-serving product in the Wrigley portfolio) and Spearmint (the most successful product in its history), which convinced him of the imperative of having strong, distinctive flavours. That commitment to flavour has stuck with the company throughout the years, the PK and Extra brands being just two of its later manifestations.

Wrigley was an enthusiast for marketing and especially for marketing communications. 'Tell 'em quick and tell 'em often', he would say. His accidental diversion into gum manufacturing only occurred, after all, as a result of a sales promotion activity for an entirely different product. He was blessed with the rare ability to spot an opportunity and act on it quickly.

Wrigley has been called the 'Father of Direct Marketing'

Wrigley's were pioneers of direct marketing and character
promotions creating the sprightly spearmen to appeal to kids.

for a very simple but clever ploy. In the early years of the twentieth century, he took advantage of the free database that the recently developed US telephone books represented and sent free samples of Wrigley gum to every address listed in them. It was the very first national direct-marketing campaign to homes anywhere in the world. Wrigley developed these direct marketing initiatives further. Two sticks of gum were sent to American children on their second birthday. A Mother Goose booklet featuring 'Sprightly Spearman', a new mascot for Spearmint gum, was commissioned. Free mascots were given to thousands of schools, particularly in poorer parts of the country where books were rare. It was one of the earliest examples of a CSR programme targeted at precisely the people Wrigley knew would want his products.

Taking Wrigley to the World

As the Wrigley business expanded, its fame crossed the Atlantic and, in 1911, William Wrigley opened his first office in Europe, at 164 Piccadilly in London. He now had more capital than his famous $32 to invest but it was still only a relatively modest £2,000. Furthermore, British social customs were not in his favour. Eating in public, even sucking a sweet in the street, was broadly frowned on. Wrigley needed people to be seen to chew its product in public in order to stimulate interest and intrigue and also to 'normalise' it as a behaviour. Sales therefore were steady if not spectacular at first.

That is, until the First World War intervened. Soldiers would chew gum in the trenches to help them stay alert and to pass the time. American soldiers brought more gum along with them when they entered the war. In 1911, Wrigley's UK turnover was £28,288; by the end of the war it stood at £188,500.

Thereafter, the social changes that were wrought by the devastation of the Great War led to a less formal, more open society and by the 1920s chewing in public was seen as fashionable, even desirable.

As well as the habit of public chewing and the strong flavours of its gum, Wrigley brought something else to the UK: its progressive attitudes to employment. Wrigley staff are referred to as 'associates' (not employees), symbolic of William Wrigley's belief that everyone should feel 'part of the business'. The company introduced practices that were advanced at the time. In 1926 it was one of the first companies to give staff paid holidays and a five-day working week. These were working practices that had already been established in the American factories and Wrigley saw no reason for not introducing them to the UK.

William Wrigley died in 1932 but his son Philip K. Wrigley succeeded him and continued the same values and approach. Philip inherited his father's commitment to people's welfare and an intelligence about turning that to commercial advantage. He took over the business just as America entered the Great Depression. Wrigley was among the first businesses in the United States to embrace the New Deal programmes of President Franklin D. Roosevelt. The company signed on with the National Recovery Administration (NRA), which created the country's first minimum wage levels. During the mid-1930s, Wrigley stationery proudly bore the NRA logo with the motto 'We Do Our Part'.

Philip Wrigley displayed such savviness again during the Second World War when he took the unusual step of removing Wrigley products from the US market. It was correctly positioned and proudly communicated as a commitment to the US troops who alone would be able to get supplies of Wrigley gum. It was also a very far-sighted piece of brand husbandry that both protected and enhanced Wrigley's reputation. Because of wartime rationing, Wrigley could not make enough top-quality gum for everyone. So, rather than compromise the high quality that people expected, the company took Wrigley's Spearmint, Doublemint and Juicy Fruit off the civilian market and dedicated the entire output of these brands to the US Armed Forces. However, following his father's legendary advice to 'tell 'em quick and tell 'em often', Philip made sure US consumers gave Wrigley the credit for its action. Throughout its absence from the US market, Wrigley ran an ad campaign which prominently featured the Wrigley packaging and carried the slogan 'Remember this Wrapper'.

The deal Wrigley agreed with the US government to be the sole supplier of gum to American soldiers overseas (there was a piece of gum in every soldier's ration pack) also proved far-sighted for the brand globally. GIs stationed in Europe were seen as glamorous and exciting. Their habit of chewing gum was associated with that glamour. When the Second World War ended and the Americans had gone home, one of their lasting legacies was chewing gum and specifically Wrigley chewing gum.

The story of Wrigley was to be interwoven again with the story of conflict in Europe. After the Second World War, Germany, and particularly Berlin, was split between the occupying forces. There was an uneasy 'truce' between East and West but with clear demarcation lines. At one stage, the disputes between the occupying forces, combined with the devastated landscape and disrupted supply lines of Berlin, meant that significant parts of the population in the zone occupied by

Wrigley's advertising in the USA during the Second World War
kept the brand in consumers' minds while the product was off the shelf.

Russian forces were running dangerously low on supplies. This caused the American-led forces to launch a series of airdrops parachuting in vital necessities. It became known as 'the Berlin Airlift'. One American pilot, Gail Halvorsen, knew how popular Wrigley's Doublemint gum was in Berlin. So, while flying aid missions, he began dropping packs of the gum using little hand-kerchief parachutes as he flew over the city. He became known as 'the Berlin Candy Bomber'. When news of his exploits reached Wrigley, they donated gum to his cause.

After the war, Wrigley achieved tremendous global success. It expanded in the UK: having built its first UK factory in Wembley in 1926, it subsequently moved in 1972 to a brand new greenfield site on the outskirts of Plymouth where it continued to invest in process innovation. And it expanded its manufacturing facilities across Europe. Wrigley now had the capacity to meet 95 per cent market share in the UK alone. It stuck to its associate-friendly principles. In addition to a guaranteed annual wage, it was the first company of its kind to provide its people with free medical benefits, sickness and accident pay, life insurance and a retirement plan. It stuck, too, to its strategy of developing products with a strong taste sensation, launching Extra Ice on its centenary. And it continued to innovate in marketing. In 1974 it was the very first packaged product to be sold using a bar code scan. Wrigley has introduced new packaging formats and new product shapes and its advertising remains fresh and stimulating.

The Legacy in Good Hands
For well over a hundred years, Wrigley was a family-run, independently owned business. Philip K. Wrigley stepped down in 1961 and his son William Wrigley III took over until 1999,

before being succeeded by his son William Wrigley IV. In 2006, William Perez became the first non-family member to run the company. Soon afterwards, the company was sold to Mars Incorporated.

Becoming part of Mars Incorporated has cultural as well as commercial benefits. It's a family-owned independent business, whose values of Quality, Responsibility, Mutuality, Efficiency and Freedom are similar to Wrigley's values. Like Wrigley, Mars is an innovative marketer whose products are features of our daily lives.

How has Wrigley done so well and sustained its success over time? Undoubtedly a belief and adherence to a few strong, clearly expressed principles has been important, creating a brand recognised all over the world. There has been a continuing nimbleness and marketing insight and foresight that has enabled it to anticipate and respond to change and to take advantage positively of any situation. It has remained committed to a culture that not only invests in and rewards innovation but also respects and recognises the people who work for it, the associates. This positioned the business as forward-thinking and socially responsible long before CEOs began obsessing about CSR. And no doubt there is a virtue, well proven here, in never complicating a successful, simple formula.

What, then, is the future for Wrigley? One of the more interesting aspects of the developing brand story over the years is chewing gum's impact on dental health. One of the original reasons that gum was mass-produced was as an aid to healthy mouth and jaw muscles. In the 1920s the brand began to seek endorsements from dentists about the benefits of chewing. Once Wrigley had introduced sugar-free gum, spearheaded by a new brand, Orbit, it had the ability to talk about the positive impact on teeth and gums, too. Orbit as a brand name no longer operates in the UK, although it exists internationally. However, Wrigley's commitment to sugar-free gum has not ceased; it has only intensified. Now over 90 per cent of all its chewing gum is sugar-free and various national dental authorities have not just endorsed chewing gum but specifically Wrigley products. The Oral Health Foundation, for example, has accredited all of Wrigley's Extra range. The benefits of chewing sugar-free gum are now officially recognised as helping to clean away food debris, neutralise plaque acids, repair tooth enamel and reduce oral dryness – a healthy list of healthy benefits.

But there could be more. Gum is a delivery base – currently it delivers taste but it could easily be developed to deliver more active ingredients for improving teeth and gums or for other health and wellbeing benefits. Think of brands like Nicorette, which use gum to deliver nicotine as an alternative to smoking. With Mars providing a range of food and drinks and Wrigley providing the gum, there may be more of a business strategy than just a brand idea in Wrigley's latest strapline.

Eat. Drink. Chew.

CONCLUSION

Martin Clarkson, who runs a business called The Storytellers, had expressed a keen interest in our venture from the off, putting his own spin on it of looking at 300-year-old start-ups. He was interested to learn what lessons there might be for today's businesses and we thought he would be a good sounding board. We arranged a meeting at The Storytellers' salubrious South Kensington office.

The office was formerly the home of war artist and portrait painter Sir John Lavery with domed studio still intact on the first floor with 'in its time, the biggest windows in London'. It certainly sparkled with the early winter light and was crying out for some large canvasses. 'Watch this space,' said Martin.

Visitors in its day had included Robert Louis Stevenson, J. M. Barrie, Oscar Wilde and George Bernard Shaw – notably Scots and Irish writers. Lavery himself was Irish and his London home provided a clandestine haven for arch separatist Michael Collins, with whom apparently Lady Lavery, svelte model in more than 400 of her husband's paintings, had an equally clandestine affair. More overtly, Lavery brought home a flower girl from Covent Garden with whom he had a child. Sadly she died but playwright friend George Bernard Shaw used this story as the inspiration for *Pygmalion*.

The house oozes history and yet sensitively incorporates pine and glass along with timeless slate floors to give the office a very contemporary feel, nestled in a Georgian shell. It's a building that reinforces the 'sense of place' that's a key aspect of our courses. Go visit a Google office, he urged, where corridors are laid out like streets and the room where people go to discuss 'issues' is furnished with ejector chairs.

The importance of culture within a business was one of the key things that Martin had drawn from our twelve stories. 'There is really deep purpose and insights behind these companies,' said Martin. 'There is more than just the product, there is a purpose within society. I know when talking to start-ups today that they're looking to do the same. They're looking at putting down roots and creating personality and culture. How deep the foundations are, I am sure, has something to do with longevity.

'Post the technological revolution nothing is left to differentiate one company from another but people and the chemistry between people. People buy products from people and what drives people is culture and belief. We come across many companies today that are facing a crisis of growth. Reinvent yourself seems to be the current mantra. But before you reinvent yourself be careful not to throw the baby out with the bathwater. In other words be careful not to throw away the company's cultural DNA.

'You have to embrace the founder's mentality. Reassert your higher purpose and know whether you're a banana or a sausage! The companies in *Established* have been through many changes and it's fascinating to read about them but I believe each has retained their cultural DNA.'

What had Martin made of *Established* as a 'business book'? 'Well, it's not a book for the businessman in a hurry, wanting the six steps to success. The lessons are hidden. It's a book to read at leisure and I think anyone in business who reads the book, feet up and glass of wine in hand, will find it charmingly reassuring. The lessons they draw from the stories will be the ones most pertinent to them. This is a book high in entertainment value and there's lots of information in the detail. The educational element is hidden though. It's a book of discovery.'

Martin's view resonated with us – that this was a book of discovery, and a charmingly reassuring one at that! But what conclusions might be drawn from our stories? What can we learn from a building, a beer, a string or two of sausages, some gum, a wine merchant's, a fleet of trucks, a few crafts, a boat, a publisher and an Aussie agricultural company?

There's no single answer – that's the beauty. The closest to a universal truth might be Woody Allen's '80 per cent of success is showing up', as we often say. But there are many insights here. And though not in any way surprising, it's their context, their emergence in a particular story, that gives them their vitality and relevance. The clue is to look for the models closest to your own. What we've drawn out here are abstracts, pointers, tips drawn from a dozen quite different stories.

Where to start? At the beginning, where else? Chances of a business's survival are heightened, it would seem from these tales, by the following: a good solid foundation and founding principles and continuing to draw from that vision and energy through the years. Even if, as Stuart Delves found with The Shore Porters' Society, the need to respond to a changed business environment takes you to a completely different kind of business. There's always value in reminding yourself how you started and how you arrived at where you are now.

It's what Richard Pelletier, in his chiselled chapter, calls a company's DNA. When floundering, look back to the original inspiration and principles and draw strength from them. Very much echoing Martin Clarkson.

'A clear sense of tradition and values, a respect for the power of story and a rebellious streak' is what Neil Baker has taken away from Berry Bros & Rudd. Believing in the supremacy of what you do or produce rather than the money. (A sentiment echoed elsewhere.) ''tis the cask, not the coffer, that holds the true wealth' is a maxim that has been passed down through the family.

And, talking about families, as the Whites told Jamie Jauncey, families need to watch out for cousins and black sheep and be alert to the pitfalls of the three-generational cycle of start-it, build-it, spend-it.

Carrying on a tradition with a very clear set of original values. Being bought by a good owner who shares the original values, as Andy Milligan says Mars is to Wrigley, adds to your survival chances. There's a really interesting example of this in the John White & Son story, where part of the new owner's challenge is to capture a 'blizzard of valuable data'. That DNA.

Answering current needs. In other words, adaptability. Being prepared to completely overhaul, as Claire Bodanis found was the case with Cambridge University Press: seizing on the spirit of the enterprise rather than the medium, being true to your purpose. Or, in the case of Wrigley, responding to the times and producing a sugar-free gum (now accounting for 90 per cent of sales).

But sometimes the need remains the same, as in the bells that Whitechapel Bell Foundry make, century upon century. If, like them, you can be unique or at least one of very few, and what you produce people still want, you're on to a winner. But there's more to it than simply that, of course, as John Simmons reveals. There's still a business to run. In the Foundry's case they took the long view, were patient, stuck to their knitting (moulding and casting) and became the best in the world. Doggedness: another slant on this. Continued usefulness, says Gillian Colhoun. It's kept Dublin's Brazen Head standing through rampage and gunfire!

The perennials. Continuous improvement. Research. Development. Innovation. Hard work. Maintaining significant relationships. Good service (the Holy Grail). Earning and keeping a reputation: and that from Martin Lee's gem of a Dorset butcher, proud of its unique history. Consistency. Consistency. Consistency. Consistency of excellence: as in a good pint today, a good pint tomorrow – just as good as the best pint ever drunk. (Guinness of course, brought to us by Guinness drinker and stalwart 'Dub' Mike Gogan.) Continuous innovation within the founder's framework: each generation finds needed solutions in different areas – science, technology, marketing, brand growth.

Shrewdness. *De rigueur* north of the border – where other qualities come into play, like being thrawn (bloody-minded) and the ability to thole (stick it out). And as with Shore Porters, kindred interests and associations, huge loyalty, equal voice.

Keeping your nerve. Especially investors, says Mark Watkins in his chapter on the Australian Agricultural Company. But it's not just nerve with muscles taut. For investors, enjoyment plays a big part. This is an interesting one. Talking recently to Peter Cunningham, head of Branding Science, his experience suggests that entrepreneurs are always interested in doing more with their money – finding a real purpose for their wealth. His client Signia Wealth, for example, provides investment advice for modern-day entrepreneurs (perhaps people who, centuries earlier, might have been the equivalents of the original founders of our companies). What he learns from Signia is that entrepreneurs want to have fun – they enjoy growing their business idea. But they're also looking for advice that is serious – they don't want to lose their money frivolously. And, importantly, they look for a meaningful approach. They want their business, their created wealth, to do something for the world that will have lasting meaning.

'But most of all,' says Mark Watkins, 'and perhaps the one we can learn most from in this age of "employee engagement", "discretionary effort" and all of those other twenty-first-century management phrases, is the fact that AACo was built on the efforts of workers who gave everything to make it a success.'

At the end of the day however, as Elen Lewis says in her piece on the eternal-hippy survivor that is the Hampton Ferry: 'Lives are lived and lost, fortunes swell and disappear. Families come and go. The floods roll in and out. The ferryman crosses the river. The river flows on and on.'

If all else fails, find a riverbank, be content with a living not a fortune.

A DOZEN *WHAT YOU DOS* TO SURVIVE IN BUSINESS

In the end, every business book needs its list of 'top tips'. Except in our case it cannot quite be done in that conventional way because we've been trying to see things from a less conventional angle. So here we set down a dozen conclusions that are drawn from this book's examples of business longevity. They are more 'things to think about' than 'things to do'.

1. Found your business on solid principles, make sure you keep those current and relevant to different times. Your origins can provide continuing guidance on what to do in the future.

2. Only persist. Better times will follow if you stick at doing what you do as well as you can.

3. There is a craft in what you do. Rejoice in the maintenance and development of that craft.

4. Be as clear as you can be with yourself about why you do what you do. Let that purpose shine through in everything you communicate about your business.

5. Respect your company's DNA. Make it part of yours.

6. Know the stories that shaped your business. Find new ways to look at them and tell them for new generations.

7. A rebellious streak can be a creative influence. Your business needs creativity.

8. Beware the pitfalls of generational drift. Fresh perspectives brought from outside can be invigorating inside.

9. Selling to new owners is always an option and not a failure. Help your buyer understand the true value of what they have bought – in the long run, culture runs deeper than physical assets.

10. Adapt to changing times because time changes everything. Embrace the need for change while remaining true to your purpose.

11. Your business is like every other; but unlike any other. Celebrate the undoubted fact that you are different.

12. Stick to what you do as long as you can be the best at doing it. But stop doing it – adapt and innovate – when it is no longer useful for the times.

Finally, although we don't have a breadmaker among our businesses, we thought we should have a baker's dozen of conclusions.

13. It is all about people – those who work for you and with you. And they all want to have meaning in their lives inside and outside work.

ACKNOWLEDGEMENTS

THANKS TO:
Alan and Kathryn Hughes for telling their story of the Whitechapel Bell
Foundry

Edwin White, Tio White and Joyce Onuonga for their help in telling the
story of John White & Son

Mike, Dave and Ben at Hampton Ferry Boathouse for their time and for
helping us cross the river www.hamptonferryboathouse.co.uk

Richard and Allison Balson

Geordie Willis
Simon Berry

Kevin Brown (The Shore Porters' Society)
Martin Clarkson (The Storytellers)
Peter Cunningham (Branding Science)

Pennie Pemberton for her help with the story of the Australian
Agricultural Company

Everyone else who has supported and helped the development of this book.

A NOTE ON THE AUTHORS

NEIL BAKER

Neil is a writer and communications consultant with twenty-five years' experience of helping people tell their stories, share ideas and make connections. A D&AD pencil holder, he has won numerous other awards for his work with brands. His clients range from global consulting firms to small, grassroots charities. He is an Associate Poet with Canterbury's Wise Words Festival and a board member of writers' organisation 26. Neil also runs workshops in creativity and wellbeing through writing.

CLAIRE BODANIS

Claire has nearly twenty years' experience as a specialist in corporate reporting and sustainability communications. She set up Falcon Windsor in 2004 to do what she enjoys most: helping her clients communicate well through words. These include plcs such as ArcelorMittal, ASOS, Diageo, GKN and Tate & Lyle, as well as public-sector bodies like the BBC and the Cabinet Office. Today the Falcon Windsor team offers a full service from strategy and copywriting to digital and print production and delivery. Claire is co-author of the Dark Angels Collective novel, *Keeping Mum*.

GILLIAN COLHOUN

Gillian is a Belfast native who began her working life in London's publishing scene, but soon dived into the bracing waters of business writing, where she helps organisations tap into their unique stories. A university guest lecturer and mentor on brand- and writing-related programmes, she has guided over three hundred companies through the cultural mind shifts of new identity programmes, content strategy and tone of voice. She is a regular speaker on the value of words in design and business.

STUART DELVES
Stuart has over thirty years' experience as a copywriter. Based in a sixteenth-century garret in Edinburgh's Old Town, he trades under the name Henzteeth. With the Arvon Foundation, then Bloom Reading Holidays, he ran over 130 residential courses. In 2005 Stuart initiated 26 Malts and in 2007 wrote *Creative Fire*, a book about Scotch the Brand. He's also a poet and an award-winning playwright. In 2014, after being Storyteller-in-Residence with Macsween of Edinburgh he brought his dramatist's skills to the service of his host client and wrote *Haggis Haggis Haggis* for the Edinburgh Fringe. Aside from Dark Angels he also runs Creative Retreats. Stuart is co-author of the Dark Angels Collective novel, *Keeping Mum*.

MIKE GOGAN
Mike is a writer, trainer and Dublin native, born under the shadow, shelter and shenanigans of the tower at Sandycove where James Joyce's *Ulysses* opens. A Dark Angel with the full clutch of courses under his belt, he has been writing to one audience or another, from one brand or another, for over twenty-five years. Day-to-day, as an in-house writer at Ireland's largest bank, he leads the change from bank language to customer language.

JAMIE JAUNCEY
Jamie has worked for many years with groups and organisations of all kinds on the power of language and stories to transform the way we see the world and our place in it. Jamie has published five novels – two of them shortlisted for the Royal Mail Scottish Children's Book of the Year Award – and has co-written with John Simmons *Room 121: a masterclass in writing and communication in business*. A former chairman of the Society of Authors in Scotland, he was for many years a director of the Edinburgh International Book Festival, the world's largest literary festival. He is also a musician and with his wife Sarah, a counsellor, runs personal development courses. Jamie is co-author of the Dark Angels Collective novel, *Keeping Mum*.

ELEN LEWIS

Elen is a writer, editor and author. She writes novels about lightning and foundlings, books about brands (IKEA and eBay), eight ghost-written books that she can't talk about and poems in the V&A Museum and Welsh National Eisteddfod. She writes and runs workshops for clients like Sainsbury's, BP, DHL, Unilever and Diageo. She sits on the board of 26, to inspire a love of language, and is the editor of The Marketing Society. Elen is co-author of the Dark Angels Collective novel, *Keeping Mum*.

MARTIN LEE

Martin is Joint Managing Director of Acacia Avenue, an agency in Islington specialising in brand and marketing advice based on market research. Like many other Dark Angels, he's also a member of 26, and is one of its longest-serving directors. His lifelong passion for books and writing found professional expression in his former role as Marketing Director at Waterstones, and nowadays his pleasure is in writing for a life, rather than a living. Martin is co-author of the Dark Angels Collective novel, *Keeping Mum*.

ANDY MILLIGAN

Andy is a founder of the business growth consultancy The Caffeine Partnership. A brand consultant since 1990, he has helped businesses around the world to define their brand promise and translate into words and actions what customers notice and value. Andy has published six business books and is co-author of the Dark Angels Collective novel, *Keeping Mum*. He has been a Plymouth Argyle fan since 1974, which has taught him invaluable life skills.

RICHARD PELLETIER

Richard began his writing life on a loud, hot summer's night in the ghetto, in a fit of inspiration, a pencil toss from the Baltimore home of H. L. Mencken, the great journalist and prose stylist. He writes for branding agencies and clients in the Pacific Northwest (his home) and beyond. With eleven fellow writers, he was a 2015 D&AD award-winner. PROUD Dark Angel.

JOHN SIMMONS

John is an independent writer and brand consultant, formerly a director of Interbrand and Newell and Sorrell. His many books include *We, Me, Them & It*, *The Invisible Grail* and *Dark Angels* (the Dark Angels trilogy) as well as books on Starbucks and Innocent. With Jamie Jauncey, he co-wrote *Room 121: a masterclass in writing and communication in business*. His fiction includes *The Angel of the Stories*, *Keeping Mum* (the Dark Angels Collective novel) and *Leaves*, his novel published in 2015. His latest novel, *Spanish Crossings*, was published in 2017. He was awarded an Honorary Fellowship by Falmouth University for services to the creative industries. He is a founder director of 26.

MARK WATKINS

Mark's career reads like a wish list of great places to live: journalism in London, corporate communications in Copenhagen and now a writer and consultant based in Canberra, Australia. He specialises in internal communications and writer-in-residence projects for clients all over the world. He has an MA in Professional Writing and is co-author of the Dark Angels Collective novel, *Keeping Mum*.

SUPPORTERS

Unbound is a new kind of publishing house. Our books are funded directly by readers. This was a very popular idea during the late eighteenth and early nineteenth centuries. Now we have revived it for the internet age. It allows authors to write the books they really want to write and readers to support the books they would most like to see published.

The names listed below are of readers who have pledged their support and made this book happen. If you'd like to join them, visit www.unbound.com.

Acacia Avenue
Kathleen Aiken Rojas
John Allert
Lisa Andrews
Dark Angels
Baillie Armstrong-Bown
Adrian Ashton
Ron Austin
James Aylett
Karen Badenoch
Shanda Bahles
Simon Bailey
Neil Baker
Robin Baker
Declan Barry
Alex Batchelor
Lucy Beevor
Nick Benson
Jane Berney
Tristram Besterman
Annie Blaber
Sarah Blackburn
Andy Blood
Lucinda Blumenfeld
David Bodanis
Claire Bonner
Marc Boothe
Rufus Boyd
Linda Brackin

Jane Bradish-Ellames
Branding Science
Mary-Thea Brosnan
Carol J Brown
Andy Bryant
Joan Buerk
Anthony Bunge
Fiona Burnett
Ken Burnett
The Caffeine Partnership
Peter Caley
Antonio Cantafio
Nick Capaldi
Jane Capper
Alicia Carey
Mathilde Caron
David Carr
David Carroll
Amanda Carson
Barry Caruth
Charlie Casey
Smiler Darren Castle
Gareth Caves
Anne-Louise Childs
Lorna Christie
Louisa Clarke
Martin Clarkson
Brian Coane
Ali Coates

Richard Cohen
Gillian Colhoun
Joan Colhoun
Robert Colvile
Kira Connaughton
Tom Connor
Ken Cox
Tommy Creaby
Creamer & Sundt
Victoria Creed
Sinead Cummins
Cathy Curtis
Rishi Dastidar
Davidovits Family
Harriet Fear Davies
Simon de Souza
Susan Deacon
Robert Deatker
Jan Dekker
Alistair Delves
Marcus Delves
Stuart Delves
Sophie Devonshire
Christopher Dodds
Luisa Dodds
Philip Doherty
Gretchen Douma
James Doyle
Jessica Driscoll

Rebecca & Vincent Eames
Ewan Easton
Robert England
Walter Enos
Ged Equi
Karen Ernberg
Roger Erskine-Hill
Susan Evans
Julius Falcon
Alistair Fee
John Ficara
Sally Fincher
Graham Fisher
Elizabeth Foley
Claire Forrest
Ellen Frankson
Jez Frazer
Ari Freisinger
Shelly Freisinger
Graham Fulcher
Amro Gebreel
Val and Nick Gibson
Alan Giles
Sarah Gill
Amy Gilliland
Eileen Glynn
Conor Gogan
Crea Gogan
Ina Gogan
Liam Gogan
Lorcan Gogan
Mike Gogan
Sam Gogan
Keith Gore
Robin Cunninghame Graham
Richard Gray
Jacinta Gregory
Chris Gribble
Catherine Griffith
Angus Grundy
William Hackett-Jones
Tim Hall
Charlotte Halliday

Simon Harper
Fiona Hart
Lynn Harvey
Eleanor Hatfield
Andy Hayes
Caroline Hayter
Daniel Headey
Daniel Herbert
Sarah Hill
Andy Hobsbawm
Gill Hodge
Marie Hodgson
Annett Höland
Anita Holford
Jonathan Holt
Roger Horberry
Jackie Horne
Adrian Hornsby
Tim Horrox
Sonya House
Jo Howard
Matt Huggins
Ross Hunter
Laura Hutcheson-Magee
Michael Imber and Stephen Cloudsdale
Sarah Isles
Paul Jabore
Daniel Jackson
Suzanna Jackson
Jamie Jauncey
Sarah Jauncey
Cathy Reid Jones
Matthew Jones
Simon Jones
Paul Jourdan
Trevor Kappes
David Kean
John Kearney
Paul Keilthy
Adam Kennedy
Christina Kennedy
Dan Kieran
Kevin Kieran

Therese Kieran
John King
Nadine Kirk
Janice Kirkpatrick
Richard Kissane
Deborah Kohn
Steve Langan
Kevin Leavy
Garth Leder
Adrienne and Brian Lee
James Lee
Martin Lee
Kirsty Leishman
Collette Lester
Kieron Letts
Alice Lewis
Alun Lewis
Elen Lewis
Jean Lewis
Tom Lewis
Jo Liddell
Magnus Linklater
James Lo
Rob Luijten
Johnny Lyons
David Machado
Sheila Machado
Seonaid Mackenzie
Jeannie Maclean
Peter Macnab
Megan MacRae
Jo Macsween
Michael Maher
Alison Manson
Janet Massey
Paul Massey
Alistair Maughan
Bill McBee
Patrick McCormack
Lisa McDowell
Stephen Mcgilloway
David McInnis
Gillian McKee
Henrietta McKervey

Shay McKiernan
Martin Meteyard
Scott Michel
Peter Milburn
Justine Miller
Robyn Miller
John Mitchinson
Mahesh Raj Mohan
Alison Morris
Damian Mullan
John Murphy
Nuala Murphy
Jane Murton
Mounzer Nasr
Carlo Navato
Michelle Nicol
Mark Noad
Isobel Noble
Kevin O'Connor
Bridget O'Donoghue
Paul O'Farrell
Cate O'Kane
Terry Oakley
David Olson
Bethan Onuonga
Brian Onuonga
Joyce Onuonga
Margaret Oscar
Raymond Parise
Simon Parsons
Lesley Pearson
Richard Pelletier
Simon Pepper
Jacqueline B Peterson
Olga Petrouchenko
Paul Pinson
Arthur Piper
Justin Pollard
Jean Polwarth
Tom Potter
Dolores Quinlan
Ilaria Ranucci
Jonathan Ratcliff
Terry Reed

Jane Reeve
Luke Reilly
Shoshana Reiman
Tim Rich
Derek Richards
Jo Rigby
David Rivers
David Roberts
Mark Roberts
Rowena Roberts
Josy Roberts-Pay
Robyn Roscoe
Karl Rudd
Jennifer Ryan
Christoph Sander
Andrew Schofield
Anne-Marie Scott
Stuart Senior
Faye Sharpe
Lucinda Shaw
Dan Shepherd
Signia Wealth Ltd
Aimee & Ada Simmons
Jessie Simmons
John Simmons
Linda Simmons
Matt Simmons
Matthew Simmons and
Mathilde Caron
Christopher Smith
David Smith
Deborah Smith
Frank & Judy Smith
Shaun Smith
Ashvin Sologar
Richard Soundy
Tim Sparrow
Martin Spencer-Whitton
Liam Spinage
Jamie Stewart
The Storytellers
Michael Strawson
Julia Stuart
Jonathan Swindley

Stephen Swindley
Ceri Tallett
Judy Taylor
Kyn Taylor
Paul Taylor
Sarah Taylor
Anne Teckman
Paul Tompsett
Elise Valmorbida
Michael Van der Gucht
Dominic Varley
Oliver Vellacott
Mark Vent
Vishaal Virani
Vivien Wallace
Bridget Waters
Mark Watkins
Craig B. Watson
Sam Webb
Joshua Welensky
Donna White
Edwin White
Tio White
Rob Williams
Joanna Wilmot
Grace Windsor
Guy Windsor
Hector Windsor
Isabel Windsor
Katriina Windsor
Rebecca Windsor
Richard Windsor
Roger Windsor
Elaine Winter
Gretchen Woelfle
Alison Woolven
Jayne Workman
Colin and Rachel Wright
Clare Yarwood-White
Sharon Young